VEGETARIAN
DINNER'S IN THE OVEN

ONE-PAN VEGETARIAN AND VEGAN RECIPES

FOR ROSS

VEGETARIAN DINNER'S IN THE OVEN

ONE-PAN VEGETARIAN AND VEGAN RECIPES

RUKMINI IYER

Photographs by David Loftus

CONTENTS

INTRODUCTION

This book includes both vegetarian and vegan recipes, which are marked with a v. Each chapter is organized by speed, depending on whether you want dinner in 30 minutes, under an hour, or over an hour—so there's something for busy weeknights as well as lazy weekend cooking. And if you want more inspiration after trying some of the recipes, the infographics in the DIY section of the book (pages 197–205) are designed to help you create your own one-pan recipe.

I was brought up in a vegetarian household—often vegan, as South Indian food tends to be. Other than pizza night, my mother rarely failed to put at least three different dishes on the table—whether it was rice, spiced potatoes, and eggplant, sambar, carrots, and beans in mustard seeds and a peppery tomato rasam; or homemade mushroom quiche, roasted vegetables, and a Caprese salad. Given that she worked full time as a doctor, I have no idea how she managed, unless I'm sublimating the memory of a lot of potato waffles and buttery macaroni with grated Cheddar (still up there on my list of favorite dinners). Food for dinner parties or birthdays was even better—homemade paneer, blitzed with spices, then formed into koftas, deep-fried, and cooked in a rich Mughal tomato and cream sauce, plus tiny stuffed eggplants, cauliflower cooked with ginger and chile, and my favorite, pulao rice with cashews and saffron.

Weeknight cooking rarely affords the time for so many dishes, so I've taken the principles of vegetarian cooking

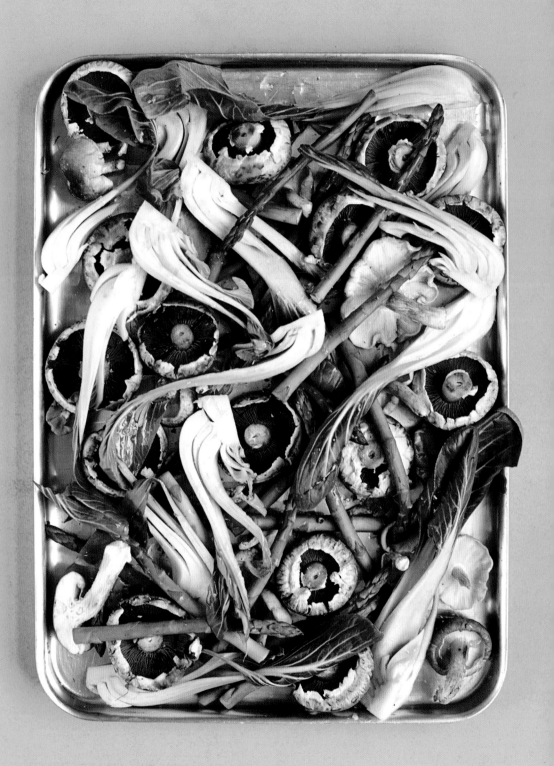

learned from home and applied them to the one-pan meals in this book. All the dishes are packed with flavor, through spices or fresh herbs and almost always lemon or lime juice (I am considering shares in a citrus farm). There's also a variety of both color and texture in each dish. Inspired by my mother's Indian cooking, there are a number of oven-roasted curries in the book, although rather than slowly frying off onions, then spices, then each vegetable, and simmering on the stove for half an hour, I've designed recipes in which everything is roasted in a single layer before adding the sauce, as with the beet, chickpea & coconut curry on page 146, which is a favorite among my friends.

Moving west, I've found that orzo and bulgur are all-in-one-pan heroes—add enough stock, layer your vegetables on top, and stick it all in the oven for just 15–20 minutes and you have a balanced dinner that needs nothing more than a glass of wine on the side. If this sounds good, try the all-in-one roasted tomato & bay orzo with black pepper (page 40) and the crispy kale & bulgur salad with pomegranate, preserved lemon, goat cheese & almonds (page 34).

This book was slightly in danger of becoming the gratin and tart book, because I love both. There aren't many things better than a hot, crisp, breadcrumb-topped gratin—the leek & French lentil gratin with crunchy feta topping (page 124) is outstanding. If you're after comfort food, try the dauphinoise/tartiflette hybrid on page 192. My boyfriend, recently initiated into the joys of ready-rolled puff pastry, finds it a revelation: unroll, top with vegetables, and bake—it's an easy weeknight win. The quick cheese & onion tart (page 86) and the carrot & Taleggio tarte tatin (page 96) are as good for midweek suppers as they are for dinner parties.

For weekends or special occasions, there are dishes that take a little longer in the oven but are just as low-effort: try the beautiful escalivada—slow-roasted peppers, eggplants & tomatoes with basil & almond dressing (page 166), whole stuffed mini pumpkins with sage & goat cheese (page 168), or whole roasted cauliflower with ras el hanout, pearl barley & pomegranate (page 170).

All the recipes are designed to work as stand-alone dinners if you wish—you'll need nothing more than a grain or some greenery for a full meal unless they're already incorporated into the dish. But if you're feeding more people, it's always nice to combine several dishes and share; you'll find suggested recipe pairings at the end of the book (page 207), with combinations that I've found work particularly well together. As with my previous book, *Dinner's in the Oven: Simple One-Pan Meals*: chop, kick back, and let the oven do the work.

A note on tablespoons: All tablespoons mentioned are the standard 15ml measure. You don't have to be exact when drizzling oil over a tray of vegetables—the amount given in tablespoons is a guideline if you want it—but a 15ml measure is useful for getting the proportions just right for the dressings in this book. All the salt is sea salt flakes.

SIDES

SIDES

Lots of the recipes in this book feature an integral carbohydrate that goes in the pan with everything else— whether bulgur, pastry, potatoes, or something similar. For those that don't, if you want a grain to bulk up the dish, here's a quick guide to cooking times if you need it: pick one that will be ready in time for dinner. There are suggestions to jazz them all up at the end of the section. All quantities below serve 4. Serve alone or with one of the flavor mixes below.

5 MINUTES—COUSCOUS: PLAIN/WHOLE GRAIN: Place 1 cup [200g] in a bowl, pour 1 cup [250ml] boiling vegetable stock over it, cover with a plate, then let it stand for 5 minutes. Fluff with a fork and serve.

20 MINUTES—QUINOA: Rinse it really well to get rid of the bitterness, pour 1⅓ cup [240g] of the quinoa and 2 cups [500ml] boiling vegetable stock into a saucepan, bring to a boil, then loosely cover and simmer for 15–17 minutes until the grains have absorbed all the water. Turn off the heat, fluff with a fork, and then let it steam, covered, for 5 minutes.

12 MINUTES—QUICK-COOK FARRO: I like farro because it has the texture of spelt or pearl barley but only takes a fraction of the time to cook. Put 1 cup [200g] in a large pan of boiling salted water, and simmer for 10–12 minutes. Drain well, and serve.

15 MINUTES—BULGUR: For the very rare occasions where I haven't specified sticking the bulgur in the pan with stock and all the vegetables, you can also cook 1 cup and 2 tbsp [300g] in a large saucepan of boiling salted water, simmering for 15 minutes. Drain well before serving.

11 MINUTES—PASTA: You know the drill: $\frac{1}{4}$ cup [100g] per person, added to plenty of boiling salted water, simmer for 9–11 minutes according to the package instructions, and drain well.

20 MINUTES—BASMATI RICE: Here's my top secret— you can cook perfect, fluffy basmati rice every time using . . . a microwave. I rarely cook it any other way. Rinse $1\frac{1}{2}$ cup [300g] basmati rice well in cold water, drain, and put in a lidded dish with $2\frac{1}{2}$ cups [600ml] boiling water. Cover, then microwave on the medium setting for 13 minutes. Let it stand for 10 minutes.

40 MINUTES—BROWN/WILD/MIXED RICE: Place $10\frac{1}{2}$ ounces [300g] in a large saucepan of boiling salted water and simmer for 40 minutes until cooked through and slightly al dente. Drain well and serve.

55–60 MINUTES—SPELT AND PEARL BARLEY: These grains take a bit longer. Either simmer $1\frac{1}{2}$ cup [300g] in plenty of boiling salted water for 1 hour or make life easier and combine $1\frac{1}{2}$ cup [300g] with 3 cups [700ml] stock in a roasting pan or casserole dish, cover tightly with foil or a lid, then stick in the oven at 400°F [200°C] for 55 minutes.

FLAVOR MIXES: Start with a tablespoon of olive oil or butter and a big pinch of salt, and then pick one, two, or more ingredients from the list below and stir it through:

zest and juice of a lemon / finely chopped cilantro/ finely chopped mint / zest and juice of a lime / toasted cashew nuts / toasted almonds / finely chopped flat-leaf parsley / roughly chopped basil / grated ginger / fried Sichuan peppercorns / toasted pine nuts

RECIPES

1 | QUICK

30 MINUTES OR LESS
IN THE OVEN

SMOKED TOFU WITH FENNEL, BOK CHOY & PEANUT SATAY DRESSING (V)

FAJITA-SPICED MUSHROOMS & PEPPERS WITH STILTON & SOUR CREAM

LIME & CILANTRO MUSHROOMS WITH BOK CHOY & ASPARAGUS (V)

SWEET DREAMS ARE MADE OF GREENS (V)

CRISPY KALE & BULGUR SALAD WITH POMEGRANATE, PRESERVED LEMON, GOAT CHEESE & ALMONDS

PANTRY PASTA BAKE: CRISPY RED BELL PEPPER & CANNELLINI BEANS WITH GORGONZOLA

ALL-IN-ONE ROASTED TOMATO & BAY ORZO WITH BLACK PEPPER (V)

RAINBOW TABBOULEH WITH AVOCADO, RADISHES & POMEGRANATE (V)

QUICK-COOK LEEK ORZOTTO WITH ASPARAGUS, HAZELNUTS & ARUGULA (V)

QUICK-ROASTED FENNEL & BULGUR WITH MOZZARELLA, FIGS, POMEGRANATE & DILL

BAKED EGGS WITH BEET, CELERY ROOT, DILL & FETA

ROASTED RED CABBAGE WITH CRISP GARLIC CROUTONS, APPLES, RAISINS & MÂCHE LETTUCE (V)

CARROT & KALE FATTOUSH: CRISP PITA WITH SPICED ROASTED CARROTS, KALE, DATES & LEMON (V)

ROASTED CABBAGE QUARTERS WITH SICHUAN PEPPER, SESAME & MUSHROOMS (V)

GREEN MACHINE, ROASTED GREENS WITH RAS EL HANOUT, BULGUR & RICOTTA

1 | QUICK

LUNCHBOX PASTA SALAD: QUICK-ROAST BROCCOLI WITH OLIVES, SUN-DRIED TOMATOES, BASIL & PINE NUTS (V)

CRISPY TAMARIND SPROUTS WITH PEANUTS & SHALLOTS (V)

SPICY HARISSA SPROUTS & BROCCOLI WITH HALLOUMI, SPINACH & COUSCOUS

CRISP CAULIFLOWER STEAKS WITH HARISSA & GOAT CHEESE

CRISPY SPROUT & ARTICHOKE GRATIN WITH LEMON & BLUE CHEESE

ROSEMARY ROASTED ENDIVE & RADISH SALAD WITH ASPARAGUS & ORANGE (V)

WATERCRESS & PARSNIP PANZANELLA WITH GORGONZOLA, HONEY & RADISHES

SPICED ROASTED CARROT & BEAN CURRY (V)

QUICK THAI OKRA WITH MUSH-ROOMS & COCONUT MILK (V)

CRISPY GNOCCHI WITH ROASTED PEPPERS, CHILE, ROSEMARY & RICOTTA

ZUCCHINI, ASPARAGUS & GOAT CHEESE TART

QUICK CHEESE & ONION TART

ROASTED CAULIFLOWER WITH CHICKPEAS, KALE, LEMON & TAHINI (V)

THE MOST INDULGENT QUICK-COOK QUICHE: BROCCOLI, GORGONZOLA, CHILE & WALNUT

CARROT & TALEGGIO TARTE TATIN

CREOLE-SPICED LEEK & MUSHROOM TART

SQUASH & GORGONZOLA TART WITH FIGS & PECANS

SMOKED TOFU WITH FENNEL, BOK CHOY & PEANUT SATAY DRESSING (V)

The peanut satay dressing works so well with the crispy smoked tofu and vegetables—and it takes just 10 minutes in the oven. One of my favorite vegan dishes in the book.

Serves: 2
Prep: 10 minutes
Cook: 10 minutes

2 fennel bulbs, thinly sliced
4 bok choy, thinly sliced
2 tablespoons vegetable oil, divided
2 teaspoons sea salt, divided
1 pound [450g] smoked organic tofu, cut into small cubes
2 tablespoons cornstarch

DRESSING
3½ tablespoons [100g] crunchy peanut butter
2 tablespoons soy sauce
2 tablespoons rice wine vinegar
2 small cloves of garlic, finely grated
¾ inch [2cm] ginger, grated
1 red chile, finely chopped

1. Preheat your broiler to its highest setting. Spread out the sliced fennel and bok choy in a single layer on a large broiler pan and mix with half the oil and salt. Toss the smoked tofu cubes with the cornstarch, then with the remaining oil and salt and scatter them over the fennel and bok choy.

2. Broil for 5–10 minutes, until the tofu is golden brown and crisp on top and the vegetables have wilted.

3. Meanwhile, for the dressing, mix together the peanut butter, soy sauce, vinegar, garlic, ginger, and chile for the dressing. Taste and adjust the sauce as needed.

4. Serve the grilled tofu and vegetables with the peanut dressing alongside.

FAJITA-SPICED MUSHROOMS & PEPPERS WITH STILTON & SOUR CREAM

I love fajitas, and this version with mushrooms is a wonderful quick dinner. You'll need to use a broiler pan to get everything cooking evenly. Have the tortillas and sour cream ready on the table so you can serve this as soon as it comes out of the oven.

Serves: 2–3
Prep: 10 minutes
Cook: 10 minutes

²/₃ pound [300g] portobello mushrooms, sliced
¹/₃ pound [150g] cremini mushrooms, sliced
2 red bell peppers, thinly sliced
1 yellow onion, thinly sliced
1 teaspoon chipotle chile flakes
2 teaspoons ground cumin
2 teaspoons ground cilantro
2 teaspoons sea salt
1 tablespoon olive oil
²/₃ cup [25g] fresh cilantro, chopped
3¹/₂ ounces [100g] Stilton
²/₃ cup [150ml] sour cream
Warm tortillas

1. Preheat the broiler to its highest setting. Scatter the mushrooms, peppers, and onion into a broiler pan large enough to hold everything in one layer, and mix in the spices, sea salt, and olive oil. Broil for 5–10 minutes, until the peppers are charred and the mushrooms have softened.

2. Scatter over the cilantro and Stilton and serve with the sour cream in warm tortillas.

LIME & CILANTRO MUSHROOMS
WITH BOK CHOY & ASPARAGUS (V)

This is perfect with rice for a light dinner when you're in a hurry. Use the biggest broiler pan you have so you can fit all the vegetables on it in one layer.

Serves: 4
Prep: 10 minutes
Cook: 10 minutes

²⁄₃ pound [300g] mini
    portobello mushrooms
¹⁄₄ pound [120g] shiitake or
    mixed mushrooms
¹⁄₂ pound [200g] asparagus
¹⁄₂ pound [200g] bok choy
2 tablespoons sesame oil
1 teaspoon sea salt

DRESSING
Zest of 1 lime plus
    2 tablespoons juice
1 tablespoon sesame oil
1 tablespoon soy sauce

TO SERVE
²⁄₃ cup [25g] fresh cilantro,
    roughly chopped
White or jasmine rice
    (see page 17)

1. Preheat the broiler to its highest setting. Spread out the mushrooms, asparagus, and bok choy in a single layer on a large broiler pan, then add the sesame oil and sea salt and mix well. Broil for 5–10 minutes, until the mushrooms are cooked through and the greens have just wilted.

2. For the dressing, mix the lime zest, juice, sesame oil, and soy sauce together and dress the grilled vegetables with it as soon as they come out of the oven. Scatter with fresh cilantro and serve with rice.

SWEET DREAMS ARE MADE OF GREENS (V)

Roasted asparagus and avocado pair beautifully with quinoa and an orange tahini dressing in this fresh, light dish that packs plenty of flavor.

Serves: 2
Prep: 10 minutes
Cook: 15 minutes

2 avocados, halved and pitted
⅓ pound [150g] asparagus
1 clove of garlic, crushed
Zest of 1 orange
1 tablespoon olive oil
A good pinch of sea salt
Freshly ground black pepper
⅓ cup [40g] almonds or
   hazelnuts
¼ pound [100g] spinach,
   chopped
1 orange, segmented

DRESSING
2 tablespoons [25g] tahini
Juice of 1 orange
½ teaspoon sea salt
Freshly ground black pepper

TO SERVE
Cooked quinoa (see page 16)

1. Preheat the oven to 400°F [200°C]. Place the avocados and asparagus into a roasting pan with the crushed garlic, orange zest, olive oil, sea salt, and black pepper, and mix well. Scatter the almonds or hazelnuts into the pan, then transfer to the oven and roast for 15 minutes.

2. For the dressing, mix the tahini with the orange juice, sea salt, and black pepper, adding a little water if needed to make it the consistency of light cream. Taste and adjust the seasoning as needed, then set aside.

3. When the avocados and asparagus have cooked for 15 minutes, add the quinoa, chopped spinach, and orange segments to the saucepan. Mix everything well, then drizzle with the dressing and serve hot.

CRISPY KALE & BULGUR SALAD WITH POMEGRANATE, PRESERVED LEMON, GOAT CHEESE & ALMONDS

This quick, flavorful bulgur salad, infused with preserved lemon and ginger, is as good for dinner as it is for a lunchbox. Thanks are owed to Rowan, this book's U.K. editor, for the idea; I'd happily eat this every week.

Serves: 2
Prep: 10 minutes
Cook: 15 minutes

1¼ cups [200g] bulgur, rinsed
2 inches [5cm] ginger, finely grated
2 preserved whole lemons, peel roughly chopped
1 teaspoon sea salt
1²⁄₃ cups [400ml] boiling water
½ pound [200g] kale or spring greens
½ tablespoon olive oil
1 heaping tablespoon za'atar
1 tablespoon lemon juice
1 tablespoon extra-virgin olive oil
²⁄₃ cup [100g] goat cheese, crumbled
½ cup [50g] toasted whole almonds
1 pomegranate, seeds only
⅓ cup [15g] fresh cilantro, roughly chopped

TO SERVE
Greek or plain yogurt

1. Preheat the oven to 425°F [220°C].

2. Mix the rinsed bulgur with the ginger, preserved lemon, sea salt, and boiling water in a roasting pan. Toss the kale or spring greens with the olive oil, then scatter evenly over the bulgur. Transfer to the oven and roast for 15 minutes.

3. Meanwhile, whisk together the za'atar, lemon juice, and extra-virgin olive oil to make a dressing, and set aside.

4. Mix the cooked bulgur and crispy kale with the dressing, then scatter over the goat cheese, almonds, pomegranate seeds, and cilantro. Serve hot, with the yogurt alongside.

Note: Za'atar is a mix of sesame seeds, sumac, dried herbs, and spices. It's readily available in supermarkets, but if you can get hold of some from a Palestinian or Israeli grocer, it'll be much fresher.

PANTRY PASTA BAKE:
CRISPY RED BELL PEPPER & CANNELLINI
BEANS WITH GORGONZOLA

This is a good, quick pantry pasta bake, and perfect for if you, like me, buy jars of roasted red bell peppers and then don't know what to do with them. You can use any cheese you have lying about—I like the contrast of blue cheese with these ingredients, but feta or goat cheese would be just as good.

Serves: 2–3
Prep: 10 minutes
Cook: 15 minutes

²⁄₃ pound [300g] vine
   tomatoes, quartered
2 cups [200g] macaroni
2 tablespoons olive oil
3¹⁄₂ tablespoons [25g] fresh dill,
   roughly chopped
²⁄₃ cup [25g] fresh flat-leaf
   parsley, roughly chopped
One 16-ounce [460g] jar
   roasted red bell peppers,
   drained and roughly chopped
1 cup and 2 tablespoons [160g]
   pitted black olives, halved
One 14.5-ounce [400g] can
   cannellini beans, drained
3 scallions, finely chopped
2 teaspoons smoked paprika
Juice of ¹⁄₂ lemon
3¹⁄₂ ounces [100g] Gorgonzola
   piccante, roughly crumbled
1 teaspoon sea salt
Freshly ground black pepper
³⁄₄ cup and 2 tablespoons [50g]
   panko breadcrumbs

1. Preheat the broiler to its highest setting. Place the tomatoes into a small lasagna dish, transfer to the oven, and broil for 5–10 minutes, until softened.

2. Meanwhile, bring a large pan of salted water to a boil and cook the macaroni or ditalini for 9–11 minutes, or according to the package instructions, until just al dente.

3. Drain the pasta, then stir in the grilled tomatoes, olive oil, herbs, red bell peppers, black olives, cannellini beans, scallions, smoked paprika, lemon juice, half the cheese, the sea salt, and a good grind of black pepper. Taste and adjust the lemon juice, salt, and olive oil as needed.

4. Return the mixture to the lasagna dish and scatter over the remaining cheese and the panko breadcrumbs. Drizzle with a little olive oil, then return to the broiler for 3–5 minutes, until crisp and golden brown. Serve hot. Leftovers are excellent in a lunchbox.

ALL-IN-ONE ROASTED TOMATO & BAY ORZO WITH BLACK PEPPER (V)

This simple dish allows the concentrated flavor of the roasted tomatoes to really infuse into the pasta, packing an intense flavor hit. An elegant, risotto-like dinner.

Serves: 2
Prep: 10 minutes
Cook: 20 minutes

7 ounces [200g] orzo
1²⁄₃ cups [400ml] vegetable
   stock
1 pound [400g] cherry tomatoes
   on the vine, halved
   (save the vines)
½ red onion, very finely
   chopped
2 bay leaves
Freshly ground black pepper
2 teaspoons sea salt, divided
2 tablespoons extra-virgin
   olive oil
A good handful of fresh basil
   or flat-leaf parsley, chopped

1. Preheat the oven to 400°F [200°C]. Mix the orzo with the vegetable stock in a deep roasting pan and lay the tomato vines over the top. (The tomato flavor will infuse into the stock.)

2. Arrange the cherry tomatoes in an even layer over the orzo, then scatter with the red onion, bay leaves, plenty of black pepper, and 1 teaspoon of the sea salt. Transfer to the oven and cook, uncovered, for 20 minutes.

3. As soon as the orzo is cooked (the pasta should be just al dente), remove the vines and stir in the extra-virgin olive oil, the remaining 1 teaspoon of sea salt, and the herbs. Taste and season with more salt and pepper as needed, and add a little dash more of stock, if you like. Serve immediately.

RAINBOW TABBOULEH
WITH AVOCADO, RADISHES
& POMEGRANATE (V)

This tabbouleh has more bulgur than a traditional version (which is mostly a parsley salad), so think of this as a hybrid. Cooked along with the tomatoes, the bulgur develops a wonderful flavor, making for a lovely, fresh grain-based dish.

Serves: 2–3
Prep: 15 minutes
Cook: 20 minutes

1¼ cups [200g] bulgur
1 cup [250ml] boiling vegetable
   stock
6 small vine tomatoes, finely
   chopped
Zest and juice of 1 lemon
²/₃ cup [25g] fresh cilantro,
   finely chopped
1½ cups [50g] fresh flat-leaf
   parsley, finely chopped
1 tablespoon extra-virgin
   olive oil
1 teaspoon sea salt
Freshly ground black pepper
4 scallions, thinly sliced
6 radishes, thinly sliced
1 avocado, thinly sliced
1 pomegranate, seeds only

1. Preheat the oven to 400°F [200°C]. Mix the bulgur, boiling stock, tomatoes, and lemon zest in a roasting pan, then transfer to the oven and cook, uncovered, for 20 minutes.

2. Take the bulgur out of the oven, give it a stir, and leave it to steam dry for 5 minutes before stirring in the lemon juice, cilantro, parsley, olive oil, sea salt, and black pepper.

3. Taste and adjust the seasoning as needed, then stir in the scallions and radishes. Top with the avocado and pomegranate seeds and serve warm or at room temperature. This makes an excellent lunch for the next day, too.

QUICK-COOK LEEK ORZOTTO WITH ASPARAGUS, HAZELNUTS & ARUGULA (V)

This pretty spring dish is perfect for a light dinner or weekend lunch with friends—and a good way to use up asparagus if you have a lot of it. Use blanched almonds if you don't have hazelnuts; you need the crunch to finish off the dish.

Serves: 3–4
Prep: 10 minutes
Cook: 20 minutes

10½ ounces [300g] orzo
3¼ cups [750ml] vegetable stock
2 leeks, thinly sliced
1 pound [400g] asparagus, trimmed and halved
1 tablespoon olive oil
1 teaspoon sea salt
Freshly ground black pepper
Zest and juice of 1 lemon
⅓ cup [40g] hazelnuts
¼ pound [100g] arugula, roughly chopped
1–2 tablespoons olive oil

1. Preheat the oven to 400°F [200°C]. Mix the orzo and vegetable stock in a roasting pan. Rub the leeks and asparagus with the olive oil, sea salt, black pepper, and lemon zest, then scatter all over the orzo along with the hazelnuts.

2. Transfer to the oven for 20 minutes, then stir in the chopped arugula, lemon juice, and olive oil. Season as needed with salt, pepper, and more lemon juice to taste, then serve hot.

Note: This dish, like most, lives or dies by the seasoning you add at the end. Adjust the lemon and salt to your taste until it's perfect.

QUICK-ROASTED FENNEL & BULGUR WITH MOZZARELLA, FIGS, POMEGRANATE & DILL

This is a beautiful dish and perfect for lunch the next day, too. Do as Chef Alice Hart suggests and buy the shorter, fatter bulbs of fennel—they have better flavor.

Serves: 4
Prep: 10 minutes
Cook: 20 minutes

$^2/_3$ pound [300g] fennel, thinly sliced
$1^3/_4$ cups [300g] bulgur
2 cloves of garlic, crushed
$2^1/_2$ cups [600ml] boiling vegetable stock
2–3 figs, quartered
9 ounces [250g] mozzarella, roughly torn
1 pomegranate, seeds only
$2^3/_4$ tablespoons [20g] fresh dill, roughly chopped

DRESSING
Zest of 1 orange plus 1 tablespoon juice
1 tablespoon extra-virgin olive oil
4 scallions, thinly sliced
1 teaspoon sea salt
Freshly ground black pepper

1. Preheat the oven to 425°F [220°C].

2. Mix the fennel, bulgur, garlic, and boiling vegetable stock in a roasting pan, then transfer to the oven and cook for 20 minutes.

3. Meanwhile, for the dressing, whisk the orange zest, juice, extra-virgin olive oil, scallions, sea salt, and black pepper together. Pour this dressing over the cooked bulgur and fennel and mix well. Taste and adjust the seasoning as needed.

4. Scatter with the fig quarters, mozzarella, pomegranate seeds, and chopped dill, and serve hot.

Note: An hour before you want them, take the mozzarella, figs, and pomegranate out of the fridge so they can come up to room temperature.

BAKED EGGS WITH BEET, CELERY ROOT, DILL & FETA

I love baked eggs: they're the perfect weekend breakfast or late-night comfort food. These started out in ramekins, like baked eggs, before I decided they'd be happier freeform on a roasting pan. The flavors in this dish are incredible—try it and see.

Serves: 4
Prep: 10 minutes
Cook: 20 minutes

⅓ pound [180g] fresh beets,
    peeled and grated
⅓ pound [180g] celery root,
    peeled and grated
Leftover beet greens, finely
    chopped
3 tablespoons chopped
    fresh dill
¾ cup [180g] plain yogurt
1½ tablespoons lemon juice
6½ ounces [180g] feta cheese
Freshly ground black pepper
4 eggs

TO SERVE
A pinch of sea salt
Fresh dill
4 slices toasted buttered
    sourdough

1. Preheat the oven to 350°F [180°C].

2. Mix together the grated beets and celery root, beet greens, dill, yogurt, lemon juice, and feta, along with a good grind of black pepper. Line a large roasting pan with parchment paper, then divide the mixture into four piles, well spaced apart, and flatten them with a spoon in the center to form a cup.

3. Crack an egg into each beet cup, then transfer to the oven and bake for 15–20 minutes, until the eggs are done to your liking.

4. Season the eggs with a pinch of sea salt, scatter with fresh dill, and serve with toasted buttered sourdough alongside.

Note: The photograph opposite shows the eggs before baking.

ROASTED RED CABBAGE WITH CRISP GARLIC CROUTONS, APPLES, RAISINS & MÂCHE LETTUCE (V)

You might not have thought of roasting cabbage leaves before, but they turn wonderfully crisp in the oven—think crispy seaweed at a Chinese restaurant. Here, the bright-purple leaves combine with garlic croutons, apples, and raisins in a lovely light autumnal salad.

Serves: 2
Prep: 10 minutes
Cook: 25 minutes

$1\frac{1}{3}$ pounds [600g] red
    cabbage, roughly chopped
    into 2-inch [5cm] pieces
$\frac{1}{3}$ pound [150g] nice bread
    (I used olive bread), roughly
    cut into 1-inch [2.5cm] cubes
1 tablespoon olive oil
2 cloves of garlic, crushed
1 teaspoon sea salt
Freshly ground black pepper
$\frac{1}{4}$ pound [100g] mâche lettuce
    or watercress
1 apple (Braeburn or similar),
    thinly sliced
A couple handfuls of raisins

DRESSING
$\frac{1}{2}$ tablespoon lemon juice
1 teaspoon salt
2 tablespoons extra-virgin
    olive oil
Freshly ground black pepper

1. Preheat the oven to 400°F [200°C]. Separate out the leaves of the chopped red cabbage so they are not stuck to each other, then spread them out on a large roasting pan all in one layer, along with the cubed bread. Add the olive oil, garlic, sea salt, and black pepper, mix well, then transfer to the oven and roast for 25 minutes.

2. For the dressing, mix the lemon juice, salt, olive oil, and pepper together, then adjust the salt and lemon juice to taste.

3. Toss the crisp cabbage and croutons with the mâche lettuce and half the dressing. Scatter over the apple slices and raisins, pour over the remaining dressing, and serve immediately.

CARROT & KALE FATTOUSH: CRISP PITA WITH SPICED ROASTED CARROTS, KALE, DATES & LEMON (V)

This lovely Middle Eastern–inspired crisp bread salad, or fattoush, is packed full of flavor and textural contrasts: sweetness from the carrots and dates, and crunch from the toasted pita bread—heaven. It makes a wonderful light dinner or lunch.

Serves: 2 generously or
2 plus 1 lunch
Prep: 10 minutes
Cook: 25 minutes

½ pound [200g] kale, roughly chopped
1 pound [400g] Chantenay carrots, halved
2 cloves of garlic, crushed
1 tablespoon sumac
1 teaspoon sea salt
A good grind of black pepper
3 whole-grain pitas, roughly torn
3 ounces [80g] mâche lettuce
1¼ cups [250g] vacuum-sealed cooked French lentils
½ cup [80g] dates, halved
2 tablespoons lemon juice
2 tablespoons extra-virgin olive oil

1. Preheat the oven to 400°F [200°C].

2. Mix the kale and carrots in a roasting pan with the crushed garlic, sumac, sea salt, and black pepper. Scatter over the pita pieces, then transfer to the oven and roast for 40 minutes.

3. Scatter the mâche lettuce, lentils, and dates over the toasted pita bread, then whisk the lemon juice and extra-virgin olive oil together and pour over. Use two big spoons to mix everything together really well, and serve immediately.

Note: If you're keeping leftovers for a lunch, remove the pita and store it separately from the rest of the salad so it stays crunchy for the next day.

ROASTED CABBAGE QUARTERS WITH SICHUAN PEPPER, SESAME & MUSHROOMS (V)

Like its fellow brassicas, cabbage becomes wonderfully crispy when roasted in the oven. You definitely want to get hold of some Sichuan peppercorns for this recipe; they are intensely aromatic and absolutely make the dish. Served with rice and a punchy sesame dressing, this is a simple, elegant dinner.

Serves: 2
Prep: 10 minutes
Cook: 25 minutes

1 large pointed cabbage
$2/3$ pound [300g] shiitake mushrooms
2 tablespoons sesame oil
2 teaspoons sea salt
2 heaping teaspoons Sichuan peppercorns, lightly crushed

DRESSING
1 tablespoon soy sauce
1 tablespoon sesame oil
$1/2$ red chile, finely chopped
1 tablespoon rice wine vinegar
2 teaspoons sesame seeds

TO SERVE
Cooked jasmine rice
(see page 17)

1. Preheat the oven to 425°F [220°C]. Cut the cabbage into long quarters, keeping the stem intact, and transfer to a roasting pan, cut side up, along with the mushrooms.

2. Drizzle the cabbage and mushrooms with the sesame oil and mix well, making sure you work the oil in between the cut leaves. Scatter each cabbage quarter and the mushrooms with the sea salt and Sichuan peppercorns, then transfer to the oven and roast for 25 minutes.

3. For the dressing, mix together the soy sauce, sesame oil, chopped chile, rice wine vinegar, and sesame seeds and then set aside.

4. Serve the cabbage and mushrooms hot, with rice and the dressing alongside or drizzled over.

Note: If you can get the reddish Sichuan peppercorns from an Asian supermarket, they're much more flavorful than the regular jarred ones.

GREEN MACHINE: ROASTED GREENS WITH RAS EL HANOUT, BULGUR & RICOTTA

This lovely all-in-one dish is really brought together by the creaminess of the ricotta at the end. If the supermarket has inexplicably run out of ricotta, substitute thick Greek yogurt. Ras el hanout can vary in heat, so if you know yours isn't very spicy, add another teaspoon.

Serves: 2
Prep: 10 minutes
Cook: 25 minutes

1¼ cups [200g] bulgur, rinsed
1²⁄₃ cups [400ml] boiling
   vegetable stock
½ pound [225g] broccolini
⅓ pound [180g] green beans
²⁄₃ pound [270g] kale, roughly
   chopped
2 teaspoons ras el hanout
1 tablespoon olive oil
2 cloves of garlic, crushed
1 teaspoon sea salt

DRESSING
Zest and juice of 1 lemon
2 tablespoons olive oil
1 teaspoon sea salt
Freshly ground black pepper

TO SERVE
²⁄₃ cup [25g] mint, finely
   chopped
A handful of toasted almonds
4 heaping tablespoons ricotta
A good pinch of ras el hanout

1. Preheat the oven to 400°F [200°C].

2. Pour the bulgur into a roasting pan and then pour over the vegetable stock. Toss the broccolini, green beans, and kale in a bowl with the ras el hanout, olive oil, garlic, and sea salt, then spread the mixture over the bulgur in the pan. Transfer to the oven and cook, uncovered, for 25 minutes.

3. For the dressing, mix together the lemon zest and juice, olive oil, sea salt, and black pepper and set aside. Once the greens and bulgur are cooked (the bulgur should be soft and the vegetables crisp), pour over the dressing, add the mint, and mix well. Serve scattered with the toasted almonds and ricotta and a good pinch of ras el hanout.

LUNCHBOX PASTA SALAD:
QUICK-ROAST BROCCOLI WITH OLIVES,
SUN-DRIED TOMATOES, BASIL & PINE NUTS (V)

I often prefer pasta with just roasted vegetables and plenty of olive oil, rather than with a sauce. This puttanesca-style broccoli works perfectly for a filling lunch.

Serves: 2
Prep: 10 minutes
Cook: 25 minutes

1 large head of broccoli,
   cut into small florets
1/2 cup [70g] pitted black olives
1/3 cup [75g] sun-dried tomatoes,
   drained (reserve the oil)
1 tablespoon oil from the
   sun-dried tomatoes
1/2 teaspoon sea salt
7 ounces [200g] penne pasta
1/3 cup [40g] toasted pine nuts
2/3 cup [25g] fresh basil,
   roughly chopped
Zest and juice of 1 lemon
2 tablespoons olive oil
Sea salt
Freshly ground black pepper

1. Preheat the oven to 400°F [200°C]. Mix the broccoli florets, olives, sun-dried tomatoes, oil, and sea salt in a roasting pan, then transfer to the oven and roast for 15 minutes.

2. Meanwhile, bring a large saucepan of salted water to a boil, add the penne, and cook for 9–11 minutes, or according to the package instructions, until just al dente. Drain, reserving a few tablespoons of the cooking water.

3. Throw the pine nuts over the broccoli, then return to the oven to roast for 10 minutes longer, until the broccoli is nicely charred and cooked through. Mix immediately with the pasta, basil, lemon zest and juice, olive oil, and reserved pasta water.

4. Taste and season as needed with sea salt and black pepper and serve warm or at room temperature.

CRISPY TAMARIND SPROUTS WITH PEANUTS & SHALLOTS (V)

This Indian street food–inspired dish combines crispy chickpeas with sprouts and a tamarind dressing. Make it a snack with puffed rice or a full meal with flatbreads or naan along with the yogurt.

Serves: 4
Prep: 10 minutes
Cook: 25 minutes

1 pound [450g] Brussels sprouts, halved
1/2 pound [200g] shallots, peeled and halved
One 14.5-ounce [400g] can chickpeas, drained and rinsed
1 teaspoon ground cumin
1 teaspoon ground cilantro
1 teaspoon chile powder
1 tablespoon vegetable oil
2 teaspoons sea salt

DRESSING
1 tablespoon vegetable oil
1 tablespoon tamarind paste
1 teaspoon brown sugar

TO SERVE
2 1/2 tablespoons [20g] salted peanuts, chopped
A handful of fresh cilantro, roughly chopped
1 teaspoon chaat masala and/or mango powder (optional)
4 tablespoons coconut or plain yogurt
Flatbreads or naan

1. Preheat the oven to 400°F [200°C]. Mix the sprouts with the shallots, chickpeas, spices, oil, and sea salt in a roasting pan, then transfer to the oven for 25 minutes, until the vegetables are crisp and browned.

2. Meanwhile, for the dressing, mix the oil with the tamarind paste and sugar. Once the vegetables are cooked, toss with the dressing, then scatter over the peanuts, fresh cilantro, and chaat masala and/or mango powder, if using. Serve with the yogurt, inside flatbreads or naan.

Note: The tamarind paste used here is the supermarket-brand kind sold in a jar, not the very concentrated paste that you will find at Asian grocery stores. If using the latter, halve the amount.

SPICY HARISSA SPROUTS & BROCCOLI WITH HALLOUMI, SPINACH & COUSCOUS

This is a quick and easy dinner, and the halloumi works so well with the spices, sprouts, and broccoli. Pile into flatbreads with yogurt and you've got a filling meal.

Serves: 4
Prep: 10 minutes
Cook: 25 minutes

1 head of broccoli, cut into florets
1 pound [450g] Brussels sprouts
9 ounces [250g] halloumi, cut into cubes
2 tablespoons harissa paste
2 tablespoons olive oil
$\frac{1}{3}$ pound [150g] spinach, chopped
A pinch of sea salt
Juice of $\frac{1}{2}$ lemon

TO SERVE
Flatbreads
4 tablespoons yogurt

1. Preheat the oven to 400°F [200°C].

2. Mix the broccoli with the sprouts, halloumi, harissa paste, and olive oil in a roasting pan, then transfer to the oven and roast for 25 minutes.

3. Stir in the chopped spinach and taste, then season with sea salt and lemon juice as needed. Serve piled into flatbreads with the yogurt.

CRISP CAULIFLOWER STEAKS WITH HARISSA & GOAT CHEESE

This is one of the most visually beautiful dishes in the book, and it tastes as good as it looks. Serve with Greek yogurt and some couscous on the side.

Serves: 4
Prep: 10 minutes
Cook: 25–30 minutes

1 very large cauliflower
1 tablespoon olive oil
1 teaspoon sea salt, divided
1 red onion, quartered
4 teaspoons harissa paste
4½ ounces [125g] soft goat cheese, crumbled
¼ cup [30g] pine nuts, roughly chopped
⅓ cup [20g] panko breadcrumbs
2 tablespoons flat-leaf parsley, chopped

TO SERVE
Couscous (see page 16)
Greek yogurt

1. Preheat the oven to 400°F [200°C]. Remove the greens from the cauliflower. Mix with olive oil and season with sea salt to taste.

2. Slice the cauliflower from top to bottom into four thick steaks and lay them in the pan along with the greens and red onion. Rub each steak on both sides with ½ teaspoon of harissa paste. Season with sea salt to taste, then press the goat cheese onto each steak.

3. Mix the pine nuts, panko breadcrumbs, and parsley with a pinch of sea salt, then scatter a quarter of this mixture over each cauliflower steak, pressing it down lightly.

4. Drizzle with olive oil, then transfer to the oven to roast for 25–30 minutes, until the tops are golden brown and the cauliflower is just cooked through. Serve the steaks with couscous and Greek yogurt, with the crispy cauliflower leaves and onions alongside.

CRISPY SPROUT & ARTICHOKE GRATIN WITH LEMON & BLUE CHEESE

Not everyone shares my love for Brussels sprouts, but this might convert the most hardened skeptic. Artichoke is a lovely pairing in this rich, crisp gratin—perfect for a cold night.

Serves: 4
Prep: 10 minutes
Cook: 25 minutes

1 pound [450g] Brussels
    sprouts, halved
$^2/_3$ 10-ounce [175g] jar
    artichokes, drained (reserve
    the oil)
1 tablespoon oil from the jarred
    artichokes
1$^1/_4$ cups [300ml] light cream
1 tablespoon lemon juice
3$^1/_2$ ounces [100g] Stilton,
    crumbled
A good grind of black pepper
$^3/_4$ cup and 3 tablespoons [50g]
    panko breadcrumbs

TO SERVE
4 thin slices sourdough bread,
    toasted

1. Preheat the oven to 400°F [200°C].

2. Mix the Brussels sprouts, artichokes, oil, light cream, and lemon juice together in a roasting pan, then top with the crumbled Stilton, black pepper, and panko breadcrumbs. Transfer to the oven and roast for 25–30 minutes, until the top is golden brown and bubbling.

3. Serve hot, with thinly sliced toasted sourdough alongside.

ROSEMARY ROASTED ENDIVE & RADISH SALAD WITH ASPARAGUS & ORANGE (V)

Serve this lovely summer salad with plenty of good crusty bread for a light lunch.

Serves: 2
Prep: 10 minutes
Cook: 30 minutes

4 heads of endive, halved
½ pound [200g] radishes, halved
¼ pound [100g] asparagus
1 tablespoon olive oil
2 sprigs rosemary
Zest of 1 orange plus 2 tablespoons orange juice
Freshly ground black pepper
2 teaspoons sea salt, divided
1¼ cups [250g] French lentils
¼ pound [100g] watercress
1 orange, segmented
1 tablespoon extra-virgin olive oil

1. Preheat the oven to 400°F [200°C].

2. Mix the endive, radishes, and asparagus in a roasting pan with the olive oil, rosemary, orange zest, black pepper, and 1 teaspoon of the sea salt, then transfer to the oven and roast for 30 minutes.

3. Once cooked, stir in the French lentils, watercress, and orange segments, and dress with the extra-virgin olive oil, orange juice, and remaining 1 teaspoon of sea salt. Taste and adjust the seasoning as needed, then serve warm.

Note: You can place a bowl under the orange as you segment it to collect the juice, and use that for the dressing rather than juice from a second orange.

WATERCRESS & PARSNIP PANZANELLA WITH GORGONZOLA, HONEY & RADISHES

The pan shown opposite didn't last very long after the picture was shot: everyone kept diving in to fish out bits of honey-drizzled parsnip and Gorgonzola. A very addictive warm salad.

Serves: 2
Prep: 10 minutes
Cook: 30 minutes

2 bread rolls (ciabatta or sourdough), roughly torn
1 pound [500g] parsnips, peeled and cut into $1/2$-inch [1cm] half-moons
1 tablespoon olive oil
1 clove of garlic, crushed
2–3 sprigs fresh rosemary
1 teaspoon sea salt
$1/4$ pound [100g] watercress
$1/4$ pound [100g] radishes, thinly sliced
$3^{1}/_{2}$ ounces [100g] Gorgonzola piccante
1 tablespoon honey

DRESSING
2 teaspoons red wine vinegar
2 tablespoon extra-virgin olive oil
1 teaspoon sea salt
A good grind of black pepper

1. Preheat the oven to 400°F [200°C].

2. Mix the torn bread, parsnips, olive oil, garlic, rosemary, and sea salt in a roasting pan, then transfer to the oven and roast for 30 minutes.

3. Meanwhile, for the dressing, whisk together the red wine vinegar, extra-virgin olive oil, sea salt, and black pepper and set aside.

4. Mix the roasted parsnips and toasted bread with the watercress, radishes, Gorgonzola, and dressing. Pile onto plates and drizzle over the honey just before serving.

SPICED ROASTED CARROT & BEAN CURRY (V)

This South Indian–style curry is a dry one, made without a gravy, so the vegetables are wonderfully crisp. Serve with coconut yogurt on the side, along with plenty of fluffy white rice.

Serves: 2
Prep: 10 minutes
Cook: 30 minutes

½ pound [220g] carrots, peeled
⅓ pound [180g] green beans, trimmed
½ cauliflower, cut into small florets
1 tablespoon vegetable oil
2 inches [5cm] ginger, grated
2 teaspoons mustard seeds
½ teaspoon ground turmeric
½ teaspoon chile powder
10 fresh curry leaves
2 teaspoons sea salt
Juice of 1 lemon

TO SERVE
Basmati rice (see page 17)
4 tablespoons coconut yogurt
A handful of unsalted peanuts

1. Preheat the oven to 425°F [220°C]. Cut the carrots in half lengthwise, then again into long, slim strips, about the width of the green beans.

2. Mix the carrots, beans, and cauliflower in a large roasting pan with the oil, ginger, spices, curry leaves, and sea salt, then transfer to the oven and roast for 30 minutes.

3. Season with the lemon juice and salt to taste, and serve with basmati rice, yogurt, and a handful of unsalted peanuts for crunch.

Note: If your local market does not carry fresh curry leaves, check your local Indian grocery store or online.

QUICK THAI OKRA
WITH MUSHROOMS
& COCONUT MILK (V)

The quick-roasted okra lends a wonderful flavor to this dish, which can be on the table in just 30 minutes. Serve with some quick-cook noodles or rice.

Serves: 2
Prep: 10 minutes
Cook: 30 minutes

$\frac{1}{2}$ pound [250g] okra
$\frac{1}{4}$ pound [125g] shiitake or
    oyster mushrooms
1 stalk of lemongrass, smashed
2 Thai lime leaves
1 teaspoon sea salt
1 tablespoon sesame or
    vegetable oil
2 cloves of garlic, grated
2 inches [5cm] ginger, grated
2 tablespoons tom yum paste
One 14.5-ounce [400ml] can
    coconut milk
$\frac{1}{3}$ cup and 3 tablespoons
    [100ml] water
Soy sauce, to taste
1 red chile, sliced
3 scallions, sliced

TO SERVE
Rice or quick-cook noodles
    (see page 17)

1. Preheat the oven to 400°F [200°C]. Mix the okra, mushrooms, lemongrass, lime leaves, and sea salt with the oil in a small roasting pan, then transfer to the oven and roast for 15 minutes.

2. In a small bowl, mix together the garlic, ginger, tom yum paste, coconut milk, and water. When the vegetables have cooked for 15 minutes, pour the coconut mixture over the vegetables, then return to the oven for an additional 15 minutes.

3. Taste and season with soy sauce, scatter over the chile slices and scallions, and serve with rice or quick-cook noodles.

CRISPY GNOCCHI WITH ROASTED PEPPERS, CHILE, ROSEMARY & RICOTTA

The gnocchi with mozzarella and tomatoes from the first *Dinner's in the Oven* book was so popular that I decided to revisit it, as there are never too many ways to eat crispy gnocchi. This version, with roasted red bell peppers and rosemary, is a lovely alternative. Use a very large and ideally metal roasting pan, for maximum crunch on the potatoes.

Serves: 2 generously
Prep: 15 minutes
Cook: 30 minutes

1 pound [500g] gnocchi
1 pound [500g] mixed red,
    yellow, and mini bell peppers,
    roughly chopped
$\frac{1}{2}$ pound [200g] cherry
    tomatoes, halved
2 tablespoons olive oil
2 bay leaves
2 cloves of garlic
1 teaspoon chile flakes
2 large sprigs fresh rosemary
1 teaspoon sea salt
Freshly ground black pepper
4 tablespoons ricotta
A handful of freshly chopped
    parsley

1. Preheat the oven to 425°F [220°C]. Place the gnocchi in a large bowl, then pour a saucepan's worth of boiling water over it and let it stand for 2 minutes before draining well.

2. Place the gnocchi in a roasting pan along with everything except the ricotta and parsley and mix well. Make sure you use a pan big enough for everything to fit in one layer. Transfer to the oven and cook for 30 minutes, until the gnocchi is crisp and golden.

3. Taste and season with sea salt and black pepper as needed, then dollop on the ricotta and scatter with the parsley before serving hot.

ZUCCHINI, ASPARAGUS & GOAT CHEESE TART

I'm fairly sure a version of this simple weeknight dinner grew out of a quick fridge raid before catching up on *Game of Thrones*, but it turned out so well that it deserved more than one repeat. By all means substitute feta for the goat cheese—it's lovely either way. Serve with simply dressed or roasted cherry tomatoes on the side.

Serves: 4
Prep: 10 minutes
Cook: 30 minutes

2 zucchini, very thinly sliced
   into rounds
½ pound [200g] asparagus
½ tablespoon olive oil
½ teaspoon sea salt
Zest of 1 lemon
Freshly ground black pepper
A handful of fresh dill, roughly
   chopped
One 10-by-15-inch [25-by-
   38cm] sheet frozen puff
   pastry, thawed
2 tablespoons crème fraîche
3½ ounces [100g] goat cheese
   with rind, thinly sliced

TO SERVE
Roasted or dressed cherry
   tomatoes

1. Preheat the oven to 400°F [200°C]. Mix the zucchini and asparagus in a bowl with the oil, sea salt, lemon zest, black pepper, and dill.

2. Lay the puff pastry on a parchment-lined roasting pan and spread with the crème fraîche, leaving a 1-inch [2.5cm] border around the edges. Arrange the zucchini slices like fish scales, slightly overlapping, on top of the crème fraîche, then lay over first the goat cheese slices, then the asparagus.

3. Transfer to the oven and cook for 30 minutes. Serve hot, with a salad or tomatoes alongside.

QUICK CHEESE & ONION TART

Shallots become wonderfully sweet after half an hour in the oven, and they make a great substitute for yellow onions in this tart. This is great as a quick post-work dinner served with a crunchy green salad.

Serves: 4
Prep: 10 minutes
Cook: 30 minutes

1 pound [400g] shallots, peeled
One 10-by-15-inch [25-by-38cm] sheet frozen puff pastry, thawed
1 tablespoon Dijon mustard
3 ounces [80g] aged Cheddar, grated
A few sprigs of fresh thyme
Freshly ground black pepper

TO SERVE
Green salad

1. Preheat the oven to 400°F [200°C]. Cut each shallot into four slices lengthwise.

2. Lay out the puff pastry on a roasting pan lined with parchment paper, and spread on the Dijon mustard, leaving a 1-inch [2.5cm] border around the edge. Arrange the flat shallot slices over the top, then scatter over the Cheddar, thyme, and black pepper.

3. Transfer to the oven for 30 minutes. Serve hot with a green salad alongside.

ROASTED CAULIFLOWER WITH CHICKPEAS, KALE, LEMON & TAHINI (V)

Cauliflower was made to be roasted, and the spices in this dish work perfectly with the tahini dressing. Make sure you use a big enough roasting pan, so the cauliflower can crisp up along with the chickpeas. An easy, flavorful dinner.

Serves: 4
Prep: 10 minutes
Cook: 30 minutes

1 large cauliflower, cut into
    large florets
One 14.5-ounce [400g] can
    chickpeas, drained and rinsed
1 large red onion, quartered
1/2 pound [200g] kale
2 tablespoons olive oil
2 teaspoons ground cumin
2 teaspoons ground cilantro
2 teaspoons ground ginger
1 teaspoon smoked paprika
2 teaspoons sea salt

DRESSING
4 tablespoons [60g] tahini
Juice of 1 lemon
2 tablespoons olive oil
4 tablespoons [60ml] water
1 teaspoon sea salt
Freshly ground black pepper

TO SERVE
2/3 cup [25g] fresh cilantro,
    roughly chopped
1/3 cup [45g] pumpkin seeds,
    toasted
Warm flatbreads

1. Preheat the oven to 400°F [200°C].

2. Spread the cauliflower, chickpeas, red onion, and kale in a large roasting pan and mix well with the oil, spices, and sea salt. Transfer to the oven and roast for 25–30 minutes, until the cauliflower is just cooked through.

3. Meanwhile, for the dressing, mix the tahini with the lemon juice, oil, water, sea salt, and black pepper, adding a little more water as needed to get a nice spoonable consistency. Taste and adjust the salt and lemon juice as needed.

4. Drizzle the dressing over the hot roasted cauliflower, scatter with the cilantro and pumpkin seeds, and serve with warm flatbreads.

THE MOST INDULGENT QUICK-COOK QUICHE: BROCCOLI, GORGONZOLA, CHILE & WALNUT

Puff pastry as a base for quiche? Yes, please. I could eat this unashamedly indulgent dish every week—it's so quick to put together. Broccoli and Gorgonzola complement each other beautifully, and get a slight kick from the chile. Serve with a crisp green salad.

Serves: 4
Prep: 10 minutes
Cook: 30 minutes

One 10-by-15-inch [25-by-38cm] sheet frozen puff pastry, thawed
$\frac{2}{3}$ pound [300g] broccoli florets, halved
$\frac{1}{2}$ red onion, finely chopped
1 teaspoon chile flakes
$\frac{1}{4}$ cup [30g] walnuts, chopped
$4\frac{1}{2}$ ounces [125g] Gorgonzola piccante, crumbled
$\frac{1}{3}$ cup and 1 tablespoon [100ml] light cream
4 eggs
Zest of 1 lemon
1 teaspoon sea salt
1 clove of garlic, crushed

1. Preheat the oven to 400°F [200°C] and line the bottom and sides of a small, deep roasting pan with parchment paper. Cover the base of the pan with the puff pastry; you want it to come up the sides to hold all the filling in.

2. Scatter the broccoli florets, red onion, chile flakes, walnuts, and Gorgonzola evenly over the pastry.

3. Beat together the cream, eggs, lemon zest, sea salt, and garlic in a bowl, then pour the mixture over the broccoli, onions, and cheese. Transfer to the oven and bake for 30 minutes, after which the pastry should be cooked and the center of the quiche just wobbly.

4. Let it sit in the pan for 10 minutes to cool down, then serve warm or at room temperature.

    Note: You can use the parchment paper that the pastry comes wrapped in to line the base of your roasting pan.

CARROT & TALEGGIO TARTE TATIN

This is a lovely tart to make if you've impulse-bought some tiny, green-topped Peter Rabbit carrots at the supermarket and are wondering what to do with them; it looks even prettier if there are rainbow carrots on offer. You don't need much more than a green salad alongside this dish for an elegant weeknight dinner.

Serves: 4
Prep: 10 minutes
Cook: 30 minutes

One 10-by-15-inch [25-by-38cm] sheet frozen puff pastry, thawed
2 scant teaspoons Dijon mustard
7 ounces [200g] Taleggio, thinly sliced
$\frac{1}{2}$ pound [220g] carrots, halved lengthwise
1 tablespoon olive oil
1 teaspoon sea salt
Freshly ground black pepper
A few sprigs of fresh thyme

TO SERVE
Green salad

1. Preheat the oven to 400°F [200°C]. Lay the pastry on a parchment-lined baking sheet and spread with the mustard, leaving a 1-inch [2.5cm] border around the edges, then scatter over the Taleggio.

2. Toss the halved carrots with the olive oil, sea salt, and black pepper, then arrange them over the cheese. Scatter over the thyme, then transfer to the oven and roast for 30 minutes.

3. Serve hot, with a green salad alongside.

CREOLE-SPICED LEEK & MUSHROOM TART

I love the combination of cayenne pepper, paprika, and lemon in this cream cheese tart base: it works perfectly with the leeks and mushrooms. Serve with some lightly dressed spinach on the side and you've got a flavorful, filling dinner.

Serves: 4
Prep: 10 minutes
Cook: 30 minutes

One 10-by-15-inch [25-by-38cm] sheet frozen puff pastry, thawed
$3/4$ cup [180g] cream cheese
1 teaspoon smoked paprika
$1/2$ teaspoon cayenne pepper
Zest and juice of 1 lemon
Freshly ground black pepper
$1 1/2$ teaspoons sea salt, divided
$1/4$ pound [120g] cremini mushrooms, thinly sliced
1 tablespoon olive oil, divided
$1/3$ pound [175g] baby leeks, halved lengthwise

TO SERVE
Green salad

1. Preheat the oven to 400°F [200°C]. Lay the pastry on a parchment-lined roasting pan and cut it down so that it is about 1 inch [2.5cm] longer at each end than the leeks (see photograph).

2. Mix together the cream cheese, paprika, cayenne, lemon zest and juice, black pepper, and $1/2$ teaspoon of the sea salt, then spread the mixture over the pastry, leaving a 1-inch [2.5cm] border around the edges.

3. Mix the mushrooms with half the oil and another $1/2$ teaspoon of salt and scatter over the cream cheese. Mix the leeks with the remaining oil and remaining $1/2$ teaspoon of salt and lay them over the mushrooms. Transfer to the oven and cook for 30 minutes.

4. Serve the tart hot, with a green salad alongside.

SQUASH & GORGONZOLA TART
WITH FIGS & PECANS

Gorgonzola and figs work beautifully with squash for a lovely autumnal dish. The trick with this tart, as with many of the squash dishes in the book, is to dice the squash into tiny ½-inch [1cm] cubes, so it'll cook through perfectly in half an hour.

Serves: 6
Prep: 15 minutes
Cook: 30 minutes

1 pound [500g] butternut
   squash, peeled and cut into
   ½-inch [1cm] cubes
½ tablespoon olive oil
1 teaspoon sea salt
One 10-by-15-inch [25-by-
   38cm] sheet frozen puff
   pastry, thawed
1 heaping tablespoon crème
   fraîche
7 ounces [200g] Gorgonzola
   piccante, crumbled
5 figs, quartered
A handful of fresh basil leaves
1 tablespoon honey
⅓ cup and 1 tablespoon [45g]
   chopped pecans

1. Preheat the oven to 400°F [200°C]. Mix the butternut squash cubes with the olive oil and sea salt.

2. Lay the puff pastry on a parchment-lined baking sheet and cut into six squares. Spread each with the crème fraîche, leaving a ½-inch [1cm] border around the edges. Scatter evenly with the squash, then the Gorgonzola, and top each serving with a few fig quarters and a basil leaf, then drizzle over the honey.

3. Transfer to the oven and cook for 20 minutes, then remove and scatter over the pecans. Return to the oven for an additional 10 minutes, until the pastry is golden brown and the squash is cooked through.

4. Serve hot and scattered with more basil.

2 | MEDIUM

LESS THAN 1 HOUR
IN THE OVEN

CRISPY GNOCCHI WITH
MUSHROOMS, SQUASH & SAGE (V)

MEDITERRANEAN ZUCCHINI
ROASTED WITH OLIVES, FETA &
TOMATOES

HERBY ROASTED PEPPERS
STUFFED WITH ARTICHOKES,
OLIVES & FETA

ROASTED TOMATO, RED
BELL PEPPER & ARTICHOKE
PANZANELLA WITH TARRAGON &
LEMON (V)

RED WINE MUSHROOM
CASSEROLE WITH CHEESE
COBBLER TOPPING·

STUFFED ROASTED FENNEL &
MUSHROOMS WITH GRUYÈRE

CANNELLINI BEAN FALAFEL WITH
POTATO WEDGES, SPINACH &
POMEGRANATE

LEEK & FRENCH LENTIL GRATIN
WITH CRUNCHY FETA TOPPING

GOAT CHEESE, PARSNIP & CARROT
TART WITH ROSEMARY

ALL-IN-ONE SWEET POTATO THAI
CURRY (V)

OKRA & CHICKPEA CURRY WITH
ALMONDS (V)

SQUASH & SPINACH CURRY (V)

EGGPLANT WITH TOMATOES,
HARISSA & ALMONDS (V)

2 | MEDIUM

HONEY-ROASTED ROOT
VEGETABLE SALAD WITH BLUE
CHEESE & SPINACH

LUXE WARM WINTER SALAD:
ROASTED POTATOES & CELERY
ROOT WITH TRUFFLE, PARMESAN
& SOFT-BOILED EGGS

EGGPLANT & FENNEL GRATIN
WITH GOAT CHEESE & WALNUTS

PERSIAN MUSHROOMS WITH
POMEGRANATE & WALNUTS (V)

MISO EGGPLANT WITH TOFU,
SESAME & CHILE (V)

CHIPOTLE-ROASTED CORN
WITH SQUASH, BLACK BEANS,
FETA & LIME

OVEN-BAKED SHAKSHUKA:
ROASTED PEPPERS, TOMATOES &
CHILE WITH EGGS

BEET, CHICKPEA & COCONUT
CURRY (V)

ALL-IN-ONE KALE & CRANBERRY
BEAN MINESTRONE WITH DITALINI,
CHILE OIL & PINE NUTS (V)

BASIL & THYME ROASTED
ONIONS WITH SQUASH,
GOAT CHEESE & WALNUTS

WARMING SWEET POTATO &
MUSHROOM POLENTA WITH
TOMATOES (V)

CRISPY GNOCCHI WITH MUSHROOMS, SQUASH & SAGE (V)

This is a lovely autumnal dish. Mushrooms and squash are a great pairing, and the sage brings it all together. Serve with a quick basil dressing for a flavorful dinner on a cold night.

Serves: 2
Prep: 10 minutes
Cook: 35 minutes

1 pound [500g] gnocchi
1 pound [500g] butternut squash, peeled and cut into $\frac{1}{2}$-inch [1cm] cubes
$\frac{2}{3}$ pound [300g] baby brown button mushrooms
3 tablespoons olive oil
$\frac{1}{2}$ cup [20g] fresh sage leaves
1 teaspoon sea salt
Freshly ground black pepper

DRESSING
$\frac{2}{3}$ cup [25g] fresh basil, very finely chopped
$\frac{1}{4}$ cup [30g] pine nuts, finely chopped
3 tablespoons olive oil
1 clove of garlic, finely grated
1 teaspoon sea salt
$\frac{1}{2}$ tablespoon lemon juice

1. Preheat the oven to 425°F [220°C].

2. Put the gnocchi into a large bowl and pour over a saucepan's worth of boiling water. Let it stand for 2 minutes, then drain well.

3. Mix the gnocchi with the butternut squash, mushrooms, oil, and sage leaves in a roasting pan large enough to hold everything in one layer. Season well with the sea salt and black pepper, then transfer to the oven and roast for 35 minutes.

4. Meanwhile, for the dressing, mix the basil, pine nuts, oil, garlic, sea salt, and lemon juice together, then taste and adjust the seasoning as needed.

5. Serve the crispy gnocchi with the dressing alongside.

MEDITERRANEAN ZUCCHINI
ROASTED WITH OLIVES,
FETA & TOMATOES

Zucchini can be unfairly maligned, but try this pantry dish and you'll have new green-vegetable converts in your house. Add a bowl of lemony couscous on the side for a lovely light dinner.

Serves: 4
Prep: 10 minutes
Cook: 35 minutes

6 large zucchini, cut into
   $1/2$-inch [1cm] diagonal slices
7 ounces [200g] feta cheese,
   roughly chopped
$2^1/_2$ cups [140g] sun-dried
   tomatoes in olive oil
1 cup and 3 tablespoons [120g]
   black olives
$2/_3$ cup [40g] panko
   breadcrumbs
Freshly ground black pepper

TO SERVE
Couscous (see page 16)

1. Preheat the oven to 400°F [200°C].

2. Put the zucchini slices into a very large roasting pan in a single layer, then cover thickly with the feta cheese. Scatter the sun-dried tomatoes and olives over evenly, then sprinkle with the panko breadcrumbs and plenty of black pepper. Transfer to the oven and roast for 35 minutes.

3. Ten minutes before you're ready to eat, prepare the couscous, stirring in some lemon juice if you wish.

4. Serve the roasted zucchini with the couscous alongside.

    Note: If you're using sun-dried tomatoes in olive oil, you don't need to add any extra oil to the dish—there's enough on the tomatoes. If you're using dried tomatoes from a package, mix 1 tablespoon of oil with the zucchini before adding the feta.

HERBY ROASTED PEPPERS STUFFED WITH ARTICHOKES, OLIVES & FETA

Stuffed peppers: retro or fantastic? As with pineapple upside-down cake, I think they are both. These lovely parcels, stuffed with rich artichokes and feta, are a far cry from the ones that turned up in school lunches, and they show us just how lovely stuffed vegetables can be.

Serves: 4
Prep: 10 minutes
Cook: 35 minutes

4 long red bell peppers, halved
    lengthwise and deseeded
One 10-ounce [280g] jar
    artichokes, drained
7 ounces [200g] feta cheese,
    crumbled
3/4 cup [100g] pine nuts
Freshly ground black pepper
2/3 cup [25g] fresh flat-leaf
    parsley, finely chopped
Zest and juice of 1 lemon
1/3 cup [50g] breadcrumbs,
    divided
1 tablespoon olive oil

TO SERVE
Crunchy green salad
Focaccia or other good bread

1. Preheat the oven to 425°F [220°C]. Arrange the halved peppers in a parchment-lined roasting pan with plenty of room around them.

2. Mix the artichokes, feta cheese, pine nuts, black pepper, parsley, lemon zest and juice, and half the breadcrumbs in a bowl, and stuff the mixture into the halved peppers.

3. Top with the remaining breadcrumbs, drizzle over the olive oil, then transfer to the oven to roast for 30–35 minutes, until the peppers are softened and slightly charred around the edges and the topping is crisp and golden.

4. Serve hot, with a crunchy green salad and good bread alongside.

ROASTED TOMATO, RED BELL PEPPER & ARTICHOKE PANZANELLA WITH TARRAGON & LEMON (V)

This is a glorious all-in-one warm salad. The sourdough for the panzanella toasts beautifully on top of the roasting tomatoes and red bell peppers, with added flavor from the artichoke oil—perfect to feed a crowd.

Serves: 4
Prep: 10 minutes
Cook: 35 minutes

1¾ pounds [800g] mixed large vine and cherry tomatoes
2 red bell peppers, roughly chopped
¾ 10-ounce [280g] jar artichokes, drained (reserve the liquid)
2 tablespoons oil from the jarred artichokes
2 cloves of garlic, crushed
2–3 tablespoons fresh tarragon, leaves only
2 teaspoons sea salt
½ pound [200g] sourdough, torn into rough chunks
⅓ pound [150g] arugula or spinach

DRESSING
1 tablespoon lemon juice
1 tablespoon extra-virgin olive oil
1 teaspoon sea salt
1 tablespoon finely chopped fresh tarragon

1. Preheat the oven to 400°F [200°C].

2. Cut the large tomatoes in half and mix them in a roasting pan with the smaller tomatoes, red bell peppers, artichokes, oil, garlic, and tarragon. Season with sea salt, place the roughly torn sourdough on top, then transfer to the oven and roast for 35 minutes.

3. Meanwhile, for the dressing, mix together the lemon juice, extra-virgin olive oil, sea salt, and finely chopped tarragon.

4. Once the vegetables are cooked, gently stir in the dressing and add the arugula or spinach. Serve hot.

RED WINE MUSHROOM CASSEROLE WITH CHEESE COBBLER TOPPING

This casserole is incredibly warming and rich for a cold autumn night. You can easily double this up to serve more people; just use a really large roasting pan.

Serves: 2
Prep: 10 minutes
Cook: 40 minutes

$\frac{2}{3}$ pound [300g] mini portobello mushrooms
$\frac{1}{2}$ pound [250g] cremini mushrooms, halved
3 cloves of garlic, crushed
2 teaspoons sea salt
1 yellow onion, roughly chopped
2–3 sprigs of fresh rosemary
1 tablespoon olive oil
$\frac{3}{4}$ cup [200ml] good red wine
2 teaspoons cornstarch
$\frac{2}{3}$ cup [150ml] vegetable stock

BISCUITS
2 cups [250g] all-purpose flour
$1\frac{1}{2}$ teaspoons cream of tartar
1 teaspoon sea salt
2 tablespoons [35g] cold butter, cubed
$\frac{2}{3}$ cup [25g] fresh parsley or basil, finely chopped
$\frac{3}{4}$ cup [60g] extra-sharp Cheddar, grated and divided
Freshly ground black pepper
$\frac{1}{3}$ cup and 1 tablespoon [100ml] milk
1 egg, lightly beaten

1. Preheat the oven to 400°F [200°C]. Mix the mushrooms, garlic, sea salt, onion, and rosemary with the olive oil in a roasting pan or lasagna dish, then transfer to the oven and roast for 20 minutes.

2. Meanwhile, for the biscuits, in a food processor or by hand, mix the flour, cream of tartar, and sea salt with the butter until it looks like fine sand, then stir in the herbs, three-quarters of the cheese, and the black pepper. Add the milk and combine everything gently into a biscuit dough. Cover and chill until needed.

3. When the mushrooms have cooked for 20 minutes, mix 1 tablespoon of the red wine with the cornstarch, then stir it into the mushrooms along with the remaining wine and the stock.

4. Form the biscuit dough into walnut-size portions and dot them over the mushrooms, flattening each slightly. Brush with the beaten egg, top with the reserved cheese, then return to the oven for 20 minutes, or until the biscuits are golden brown and crisp, and the sauce is thick and reduced. Let the dish sit for 5 minutes, then serve hot.

STUFFED ROASTED FENNEL & MUSHROOMS WITH GRUYÈRE

Fennel is a divisive ingredient in my kitchen: I like it, my boyfriend doesn't. (He has been known to pick all the fennel out of dishes that I've asked him to try for this book.) This dish has hidden fennel in the mushrooms, and more obvious fennel for the rest of us.

Serves: 2
Prep: 15 minutes
Cook: 40 minutes

2 plump fennel bulbs, halved
$\frac{1}{3}$ pound [150g] cremini mushrooms, finely chopped
$2\frac{1}{2}$ ounces [75g] Gruyère cheese, grated
$\frac{1}{4}$ cup [15g] fresh tarragon, finely chopped
Zest of 1 lemon
1 teaspoon sea salt
Freshly ground black pepper
4 portobello mushrooms, stems removed
$\frac{2}{3}$ cup [40g] panko
1 tablespoon olive oil

TO SERVE
Green salad
Crusty bread

1. Preheat the oven to 400°F [200°C]. Carefully cut out the center of each fennel bulb, leaving a "shell" behind. Chop the fennel you took out and mix it with the chopped mushrooms, Gruyère, tarragon, lemon zest, sea salt, and black pepper.

2. Stuff this mixture into the fennel shells and the portobello mushroom caps, then cover each with the panko breadcrumbs. Drizzle with the olive oil, then transfer to the oven and roast for 40 minutes, until the tops are golden brown and crisp.

3. Serve with a salad and crusty bread alongside.

CANNELLINI BEAN FALAFEL WITH POTATO WEDGES, SPINACH & POMEGRANATE

A little bit of effort is required before sticking these in the roasting pan, but it's worth it. They are lovely for a light, snacky dinner or as a starter.

Serves: 2–3
Prep: 10 minutes
Cook: 40 minutes

One 14.5-ounce [400g] can cannellini beans
$\frac{1}{2}$ clove of garlic, crushed
$\frac{1}{2}$ cup [50g] scallion, finely chopped
7 ounces [200g] feta cheese, crumbled
2 teaspoons smoked paprika
2 sweet potatoes, peeled and cut into small wedges
1 tablespoon olive oil
$\frac{1}{2}$ teaspoon sea salt

TO SERVE
$\frac{1}{3}$ pound [150g] baby spinach leaves
1 pomegranate, seeds only
4 tablespoons plain yogurt

1. Preheat the oven to 400°F [200°C]. Pulse the cannellini beans, garlic, scallion, feta, and smoked paprika in a food processor until you have a rough, sticky mixture.

2. Place the sweet potato wedges in a large roasting pan and mix with the olive oil and sea salt. Take walnut-size portions of the falafel mix and roll them into balls, then tuck them around the sweet potato wedges.

3. Transfer to the oven and roast for 40 minutes, until the sweet potatoes are cooked through and the falafel are golden brown on top.

4. Serve with the spinach, pomegranate seeds, and plain yogurt alongside.

Note: The falafel mix won't get sufficiently sticky if you try to mix it by hand, so please use a food processor.

LEEK & FRENCH LENTIL GRATIN WITH CRUNCHY FETA TOPPING

This filling gratin with its crisp feta topping is perfect comfort food—the dining equivalent of sitting cozily on the sofa under a blanket. It's good for batch cooking for the week ahead, as any leftovers will keep well for a couple of days in the fridge. This dish is a favorite among friends who helped me try out the recipes for this book.

Serves: 4 generously
Prep: 10 minutes
Cook: 40 minutes

2 tablespoons [30g] butter
3 cloves of garlic, crushed
1 pound [500g] leeks, thinly
   sliced
2 teaspoons sea salt, divided
Freshly ground black pepper
$2\frac{1}{2}$ cups [500g] vacuum-sealed
   cooked French lentils
$1\frac{1}{4}$ cups [300ml] crème fraîche
$4\frac{1}{2}$ ounces [125g] feta cheese,
   crumbled
$\frac{3}{4}$ cup and 1 tablespoon [50g]
   panko
1 tablespoon olive oil

1. Preheat the oven to 400°F [200°C]. Put the butter and garlic into a roasting pan and place in the oven to melt while you slice the leeks.

2. Mix the sliced leeks with the melted garlic butter, season with the sea salt and black pepper to taste, then return to the oven to roast for 20 minutes.

3. After 20 minutes, stir in the French lentils, crème fraîche, and another good scatter of sea salt, then top with the feta cheese and panko breadcrumbs. Drizzle with the olive oil, then return to the oven for an additional 20–25 minutes, until golden brown on top.

4. Serve the gratin hot alongside a green salad with mustard-based or balsamic dressing.

GOAT CHEESE, PARSNIP & CARROT TART WITH ROSEMARY

I'm not going to deny it: this is a time-consuming dish—in the way that making dolmas and shaping kibbeh is time-consuming—but it's worth it. If you feel like a bit of kitchen puttering, this is the dish for you. There's something curiously soothing about the repetitive ribbon rolling, and it tastes as good as it looks.

Serves: 4
Prep: 30 minutes
Cook: 40 minutes

One 10-by-15-inch [25-by-38cm] sheet frozen puff pastry, thawed
2 tablespoons crème fraîche
7 ounces [200g] mild goat cheese, finely crumbled
2–3 large carrots, peeled
2–3 large parsnips, peeled
1 tablespoon olive oil
2 teaspoons sea salt
Freshly ground black pepper
A few sprigs of fresh rosemary

1. Preheat the oven to 400°F [200°C]. Unroll the puff pastry onto a large roasting pan, then spread with the crème fraîche, leaving a 1-inch [2.5cm] border around the edge. Scatter over the crumbled cheese.

2. Using a vegetable peeler, peel the carrots and parsnips into long ribbons and transfer them to a large bowl. Dress with the olive oil, sea salt, and black pepper, then roll each ribbon into a small cylinder. Push each cylinder into the goat cheese as you go, roughly alternating the white and orange, until the cheese is completely covered in parsnip and carrot roses.

3. Congratulate yourself on a job well done, then scatter the tart with a little rosemary, transfer to the oven, and roast for 40 minutes. Serve hot, with a green salad alongside.

ALL-IN-ONE SWEET POTATO THAI CURRY (V)

For me this is the perfect one-pot dish—everything in at the same time, then a gentle, even stint in the oven, like a casserole but quicker. The flavors of the coconut, lemongrass, and chile combine well in this comforting, soupy noodle dish.

Serves: 2
Prep: 5 minutes
Cook: 45 minutes

1^2/$_3$ pounds [750g] sweet potatoes, peeled and cut into 1/2 inch [1cm] slices
1 stalk of lemongrass, smashed
2 inches [5cm] ginger, grated
2 cloves of garlic, grated
1 large red chile, halved lengthwise
One 14.5-ounce [400ml] can coconut milk, stirred
2 cups [500ml] boiling vegetable stock
1/2 package of 2-ounce [140g] fine prepared Asian-style noodles
Juice of 1 lime
2/3 cup [25g] fresh cilantro, leaves only

1. Preheat the oven to 400°F [200°C].

2. Place the sweet potatoes, lemongrass, ginger, garlic, chile, coconut milk, and stock into a deep roasting pan or casserole dish, then transfer to the oven and cook, uncovered, for 45 minutes.

3. Poke the sweet potato to make sure it is soft throughout, and then remove the dish from the oven. Immediately add the prepared noodles and submerge them in the liquid. Let them sit for 5 minutes, then stir in the lime juice.

4. Scatter over the cilantro and serve immediately in deep soup bowls.

Note: This dish is going to generate some steam in your oven, so keep your face well back when you open the oven door after 45 minutes. I speak from experience, misty glasses and all.

OKRA & CHICKPEA CURRY WITH ALMONDS (V)

Okra has a reputation for becoming gelatinous in stews or curries, but in this oven-roasted dish it keeps its form perfectly. Serve this warming curry with rice and vegan yogurt.

Serves: 2
Prep: 10 minutes
Cook: 45 minutes

1 tablespoon vegetable oil
1 yellow onion, roughly chopped
$\frac{1}{2}$ pound [250g] okra
1 heaping teaspoon ground cumin
1 teaspoon ground cilantro
$\frac{1}{2}$ teaspoon ground turmeric
$\frac{1}{2}$ teaspoon chile powder
1 teaspoon smoked paprika
1 teaspoon sea salt
One 14.5-ounce [400g] can chickpeas, drained and rinsed
2 cloves of garlic, grated
$\frac{1}{2}$ inch [1cm] ginger, grated
One 14.5-ounce [400g] can diced tomatoes
$\frac{3}{4}$ cup and 1 tablespoon [200ml] water
Juice of $\frac{1}{2}$ lemon

TO SERVE
A handful of sliced almonds
A handful of fresh cilantro, chopped
Basmati rice (see page 17)
Vegan yogurt

1. Preheat the oven to 425°F [220°C].

2. Mix the oil, onion, okra, spices, sea salt and chickpeas in a roasting pan, then transfer to the oven and roast for 20 minutes.

3. Meanwhile, mix the garlic, ginger, tomatoes, and water together and set aside.

4. Once the okra has cooked for 20 minutes, add the spiced tomato water, stir, and then return the pan to the oven and cook, uncovered, for 20 minutes.

5. Taste and season with lemon juice and more salt as needed. Scatter over the sliced almonds and cilantro and serve hot with rice and yogurt.

SQUASH & SPINACH CURRY (V)

Serve this wonderfully filling curry with fluffy white rice or naan and vegan yogurt.

Serves: 4
Prep: 10 minutes
Cook: 45 minutes

1 medium butternut squash,
    peeled and cut into 1/2-inch
    [1cm] chunks
2 white onions, roughly chopped
2 cloves of garlic, crushed
2 inches [5cm] ginger, grated
1 red chile, deseeded and finely
    chopped
2 teaspoons ground cumin
2 teaspoons ground cilantro
1/2 teaspoon ground turmeric
1 tablespoon vegetable oil
2 teaspoons sea salt
1/3 pound [150g] spinach,
    roughly chopped
One 14.5-ounce [400g] can
    diced tomatoes
1 2/3 cups [400ml] boiling water
Juice of 1 lemon
A handful of fresh cilantro,
    roughly chopped

TO SERVE
Basmati rice (see page 17)
Naan bread

1. Preheat the oven to 425°F [220°C].

2. Place the squash and onions into a roasting pan, then mix with the garlic, ginger, chile, spices, oil, and sea salt. Transfer to the oven and roast for 25 minutes.

3. Stir in the chopped spinach, diced tomatoes, and boiling water, then return to the oven for 20 minutes longer.

4. Taste and season with lemon juice and more salt as needed, then scatter over the cilantro and serve with rice or naan.

EGGPLANT WITH TOMATOES, HARISSA & ALMONDS (V)

I could do a whole chapter on roasted eggplant, but as other vegetables are available, I've toned it down. This simple harissa-spiced eggplant dish is wonderfully filling and works perfectly with a bowl of lemony couscous.

Serves: 4
Prep: 10 minutes
Cook: 45 minutes

2 eggplant, cut into ½-inch [1cm] slices
1 tablespoon [21g] harissa paste
2½ tablespoons olive oil, divided
1 red onion, sliced into thick half-moons
8 large vine tomatoes, halved
1 teaspoon sea salt
⅓ cup [40g] sliced almonds
⅔ cup [25g] fresh cilantro, chopped

TO SERVE
Couscous (see page 16)
Plain or dairy-free yogurt

1. Preheat the oven to 400°F [200°C].

2. Lay the eggplant slices in a roasting pan large enough to hold them all in one layer, then brush each side with the harissa paste and 2 tablespoons of the oil. Mix the red onion with the remaining ½ tablespoon olive oil, then scatter the slices over the eggplant.

3. Tuck the tomato halves around the eggplant, season everything with sea salt, then transfer to the oven and roast for 30 minutes. Sprinkle over the almonds, then return to the oven for 15 minutes longer, until the eggplant is cooked through.

4. Scatter with the cilantro and serve with couscous and yogurt alongside.

HONEY-ROASTED ROOT VEGETABLE SALAD WITH BLUE CHEESE & SPINACH

This warming winter salad works well as a light main for two, or alongside a more substantial grain-based dish.

Serves: 4
Prep: 10 minutes
Cook: 45 minutes

1 pound [440g] carrots, peeled and cut into ¼-inch [5mm] slices
1 pound [500g] parsnips, peeled and cut into ¼-inch [5mm] slices
1 pound [500g] celery root, peeled and cut into ¼-inch [5mm] wedges
2 teaspoons paprika
2 tablespoons olive oil
2 inches [5cm] ginger, grated
2 teaspoons sea salt
1 tablespoon honey
½ cup [45g] walnuts, roughly chopped
¼ pound [100g] baby spinach leaves
3½ ounces [100g] blue cheese of your choice

DRESSING
2 teaspoons red wine vinegar
1 tablespoon extra-virgin olive oil
1 teaspoon sea salt
Freshly ground black pepper

1. Preheat the oven to 425°F [220°C].

2. Mix the carrots, parsnips, and celery root in a roasting pan along with the paprika, oil, ginger, and salt, then transfer to the oven and roast for 40 minutes.

3. Drizzle everything with the honey, add the walnuts, then return to the oven for 5 minutes.

4. Meanwhile, for the dressing, whisk the red wine vinegar with the extra-virgin olive oil, sea salt, and black pepper.

5. Once the vegetables are done, give them 5 minutes to cool down, then add the spinach and blue cheese to the roasting pan along with the dressing and mix well. Taste and adjust the salt or honey as needed and serve immediately.

LUXE WARM WINTER SALAD: ROASTED POTATOES & CELERY ROOT WITH TRUFFLE, PARMESAN & SOFT-BOILED EGGS

This rich dish is filled with Parmesan, egg, and walnuts—complete with roasted potatoes for a hearty meal. The celery root adds freshness, and there's a pepper flavor from the watercress—a perfect combination. You can easily cook the eggs in the pan for the last 10 minutes, as with the roast potato hash on page 174, but I prefer the look and texture of soft-boiled eggs with this dish.

Serves: 4
Prep: 10 minutes
Cook: 45 minutes

1 pound [500g] Yukon gold
    potatoes, peeled and cut into
    1-inch [2.5cm] chunks
1 pound [500g] celery root,
    peeled and cut into 1-inch
    [2.5cm] chunks
3 cloves of garlic
1 tablespoon olive oil
1 teaspoon sea salt
Freshly ground black pepper
4 free-range eggs,
    at room temperature
$\frac{1}{4}$ pound [100g] watercress,
    roughly chopped
$\frac{1}{2}$ cup [50g] walnuts, toasted
1 ounce [30g] Parmesan, shaved

DRESSING
2 tablespoons olive oil
$\frac{1}{2}$ tablespoon lemon juice
1 teaspoon good-quality
    truffle oil
1 teaspoon sea salt
Freshly ground black pepper

1. Preheat the oven to 400°F [200°C]. Place the potatoes, celery root, and garlic into a roasting pan and mix well with the olive oil, sea salt, and black pepper. Transfer to the oven and roast for 45 minutes, until the potatoes are crisp and cooked through.

2. Mix all the dressing ingredients together. Truffle oil comes in varying strengths, so you may wish to add a little more, along with the lemon juice, a drop at a time until you're happy with the taste.

3. Just before the potatoes are ready, bring a pan of water to a boil, then gently lower in the eggs and cook for 4–5 minutes for a runny yolk. Remove to a bowl of cold water and peel when cool enough to handle. Slice in half lengthwise.

4. Mix the potatoes with the chopped watercress and top with the halved boiled eggs. Drizzle the dressing over everything, scatter over the walnuts and Parmesan, and serve hot.

EGGPLANT & FENNEL GRATIN
WITH GOAT CHEESE & WALNUTS

Eggplant is often paired with a tomato sauce in a gratin, but it works beautifully with crème fraîche, goat cheese, and nutmeg in this warming layered fennel dish. The walnuts add extra crunch and flavor to the golden panko topping.

Serves: 4
Prep: 15 minutes
Cook: 45 minutes

2 cups [500ml] crème fraîche
2 teaspoons sea salt
Freshly ground black pepper
$2/3$ cup [25g] fresh flat-leaf
   parsley, finely chopped
1 teaspoon grated nutmeg
2 medium eggplant, thinly
   sliced into rounds
$2/3$ pound [300g] fennel, thinly
   sliced
$4^1/2$ ounces [125g] soft goat
   cheese, crumbled and divided
$3/4$ cup [50g] panko
$1/2$ cup [50g] walnuts, roughly
   chopped
1 tablespoon olive oil

TO SERVE
Crusty bread

1. Preheat the oven to 400°F [200°C]. Mix the crème fraîche with the sea salt, black pepper, parsley, and nutmeg.

2. Place half of the eggplant slices into a roasting pan, followed by half the fennel and half the crème fraîche and goat cheese. Repeat these layers, then scatter the top layer of crème fraîche and cheese with the panko bread-crumbs and walnuts.

3. Drizzle with the olive oil, then transfer to the oven and bake for 45 minutes, until the top is golden brown and crisp, and the gratin is bubbling.

4. Let it sit for 10 minutes to cool down before serving with plenty of crusty bread.

   Note: To get the fennel sliced really thinly, you can carefully use a mandoline or the slicing blade on a food processor.

PERSIAN MUSHROOMS WITH POMEGRANATE & WALNUTS (V)

This dish is a vegetarian version of my favorite Persian dish, fesenjan stew. There's such an amazing depth of flavor from the pomegranate molasses and ground walnuts, and if you have time, it's well worth toasting the walnuts in the oven for 10 minutes before starting the recipe. If not, this is delicious as is. Serve with rice or couscous.

Serves: 4
Prep: 10 minutes
Cook: 45 minutes

1⅓ pounds [600g] cremini mushrooms
2 yellow onions, finely chopped
1 tablespoon olive oil
1 teaspoon sea salt
Freshly ground black pepper
¾ cup [75g] walnuts, roughly chopped, divided
⅓ cup [75ml] pomegranate molasses
⅜ cup and 1 tablespoon [100ml] vegetable stock
1 teaspoon dark brown sugar
1 pomegranate, seeds only
A handful of fresh cilantro, chopped

TO SERVE
Couscous (see page 16)
Rice (see page 17)

1. Preheat the oven to 400°F [200°C].

2. Mix the mushrooms, onions, olive oil, sea salt, and black pepper in a roasting pan, then transfer to the oven to roast for 20 minutes.

3. Meanwhile, grind half of the walnuts in a spice grinder (if you have toasted them, let them cool down before blitzing) until finely ground. Mix with the pomegranate molasses, vegetable stock, and dark brown sugar. When the mushrooms have cooked for 20 minutes, stir in the pomegranate sauce, then return to the oven for 25 minutes.

4. Scatter with the remaining walnuts, pomegranate seeds, and cilantro before serving with rice or couscous.

MISO EGGPLANT WITH TOFU, SESAME & CHILE (V)

Miso eggplant seems to be all the rage at the moment, and with good reason—the flavors work beautifully together. This version adds a punchy sesame and lime dressing to liven up both the eggplant and the crispy tofu. Serve alongside fluffy white rice.

Serves: 4
Prep: 10 minutes
Cook: 45 minutes

2 eggplants, halved lengthwise
1/2 pound [250g] firm organic
    tofu, cut into 1/2-inch [1cm]
    slices
5 tablespoons [75g] miso paste
2 tablespoons sesame oil,
    divided
1 inch [2.5cm] ginger, grated
2 cloves of garlic, crushed
1/4 pound [100g] kale, thickly
    sliced

DRESSING
1 red chile, finely chopped
3/4 inch [2cm] ginger, grated
2 cloves of garlic, grated
Zest and juice of 2 limes
2 tablespoons soy sauce
2 tablespoons sesame oil
3 scallions, thinly sliced

TO SERVE
2 tablespoons sesame seeds
White rice (see page 17)

1. Preheat the oven to 400°F [200°C]. Cut deep crosshatches into each eggplant half, then transfer to a roasting pan along with the tofu.

2. Mix the miso paste with 1 tablespoon of the sesame oil, ginger, and garlic, then rub this into everything in the roasting pan. Transfer to the oven and roast for 25 minutes. Then, rub the kale with the remaining 1 tablespoon sesame oil, add it to the pan, and cook for 20 minutes longer.

3. Meanwhile, for the dressing, mix the chile, ginger, garlic, lime zest and juice, soy sauce, sesame oil, and scallions together. Pour this dressing over the eggplant and tofu as soon as it comes out of the oven, then scatter with the sesame seeds. Serve hot with rice alongside.

CHIPOTLE-ROASTED CORN WITH SQUASH, BLACK BEANS, FETA & LIME

This dish feels like a festival to me, with all its bright colors and textures: crispy black beans, soft feta, spiced squash, and roasted corn on the cob. Serve as part of a Mexican-style feast, or on its own with cilantro rice.

Serves: 4
Prep: 10 minutes
Cook: 45 minutes

1$^2/_3$ pounds [750g] squash, cut into $^1/_2$-inch [1cm] slices
4 ears corn on the cob, husks and silks removed
One 14.5-ounce [400g] can black beans, drained and rinsed
1 teaspoon chipotle chile flakes
1 teaspoon ground cilantro
1 teaspoon ground cumin
1 teaspoon sea salt
2 tablespoons olive oil
Juice of 1 lime
7 ounces [200g] feta cheese, crumbled
$^2/_3$ cup [25g] fresh cilantro, finely chopped
2 scallions, finely chopped

TO SERVE
4 heaping tablespoons sour cream
Cilantro rice (see page 17)

1. Preheat the oven to 400°F [200°C].

2. Mix together the squash, corn, and black beans in a roasting pan along with the spices, sea salt, and olive oil, then transfer to the oven and roast for 45 minutes.

3. Squeeze the lime juice over the vegetables, then scatter the feta, cilantro, and scallions on top. Serve with the sour cream and rice alongside.

OVEN-BAKED SHAKSHUKA: ROASTED PEPPERS, TOMATOES & CHILE WITH EGGS

I love shakshuka, but I don't love how long it takes to carefully fry large quantities of onions, peppers, and tomatoes on the stove. Cue the oven version: roast all the vegetables first and save yourself 20 minutes of stirring. This is a standard weekend breakfast at home.

Serves: 4
Prep: 15 minutes
Cook: 45 minutes

1 red onion, roughly chopped
2 red bell peppers, roughly chopped
2 yellow bell peppers, roughly chopped
$2/3$ pound [300g] vine tomatoes, quartered
2 red chiles, deseeded and roughly chopped
2 cloves of garlic, crushed
1 tablespoon olive oil
1 teaspoon sea salt
1 teaspoon ground cumin
1 teaspoon ground cilantro
$1\frac{1}{2}$ teaspoons smoked paprika
One 14.5-ounce [400g] can diced tomatoes
4 free-range eggs
1 tablespoon za'atar (optional)
Freshly chopped cilantro

TO SERVE
Buttered toast or pita bread

1. Preheat the oven to 400°F [200°C].

2. Mix the onion, peppers, vine tomatoes, chiles, and garlic with the oil, sea salt, and spices in a large roasting pan, then transfer to the oven and roast for 30 minutes.

3. Lower the temperature to 350°F [180°C]. Squash the cooked tomatoes down with a wooden spoon, then add the canned tomatoes and mix everything together. Make four indentations in the tomato mixture, crack an egg into each, then return to the oven for an additional 10 minutes, or until the eggs are cooked to your liking.

4. Sprinkle with the za'atar, if using, and the freshly chopped cilantro. Serve with lots of hot buttered toast or pita bread.

Note: The eggs will take more or less time depending on whether they're cold from the fridge or at room temperature.

BEET, CHICKPEA
& COCONUT CURRY (V)

Roasted spiced beets and chickpeas form the base for this dish, while the coconut milk reduces down quickly in a hot oven to make a simple and delicious curry sauce. Serve with rice or naan to create a filling meal.

Serves: 2
Prep: 15 minutes
Cook: 50 minutes

1 yellow onion, roughly chopped
1$\frac{1}{3}$ pounds [600g] beets, peeled and cut into small wedges
One 14.5-ounce [400g] can chickpeas, drained and rinsed
2 cloves of garlic, crushed
2 inches [5cm] ginger, grated
1 red chile, roughly chopped
1 heaping teaspoon ground cumin
1 heaping teaspoon ground cilantro
1 heaping teaspoon ground ginger
$\frac{1}{2}$ teaspoon ground turmeric
1 tablespoon vegetable oil
1 teaspoon sea salt
One 14.5-ounce [400ml] can coconut milk

TO SERVE
Basmati rice (see page 17) or naan
A handful of fresh cilantro
Coconut flakes (optional)

1. Preheat the oven to 400°F [200°C].

2. Mix the onion, beets, and chickpeas in a roasting pan with the garlic, ginger, chile, spices, oil, and sea salt, then transfer to the oven and roast for 40 minutes.

3. Give the coconut milk a good stir, then pour it over the beets and mix well. Return the roasting pan to the oven for 10 minutes.

4. Taste and season with more salt as needed and serve with rice or naan, and scattered with fresh cilantro and coconut flakes, if using.

Note: You might want to use gloves while you're preparing the beets, to avoid stained hands.

ALL-IN-ONE KALE & CRANBERRY BEAN MINESTRONE WITH DITALINI, CHILE OIL & PINE NUTS (V)

This is a hearty stew where the longer it sits, the more stewlike it will become. You can use any strong-flavored herbs, such as rosemary, thyme, and oregano.

Serves: 2
Prep: 15 minutes
Cook: 50 minutes

1/4 pound [100g] ditalini
1 yellow onion, roughly chopped
1 small carrot, chopped
1 stalk celery, chopped
2 cloves of garlic, crushed
2 teaspoons smoked paprika
One 14.5-ounce [400g] can diced tomatoes
3 cups [700ml] boiling vegetable stock
1 tablespoon olive oil
One 14.5-ounce [400g] can cranberry beans, drained
1/3 pound [150g] kale, roughly chopped
1 heaping teaspoon sea salt
A good grind of black pepper

CHILE OIL
3 tablespoons olive oil
2 teaspoons chile flakes

TO SERVE
Juice of 1/2 lemon
A handful of toasted pine nuts
A handful of fresh basil leaves

1. Preheat the oven to 400°F [200°C].

2. Mix all the ingredients in a deep roasting pan, then cover tightly with foil, transfer to the oven, and cook for 50 minutes.

3. Meanwhile, make the chile oil. Heat the olive oil in a small pan and add the chile flakes. Let it simmer over medium heat for 30 seconds, then take the pan off the heat. Let the oil infuse while the minestrone cooks.

4. Remove the roasting pan from the oven and let it sit for 10 minutes, uncovered, then taste and adjust the sea salt, black pepper, and lemon juice—you will need plenty of all of them. Serve drizzled with the chile oil and scattered with the pine nuts and basil leaves.

Note: Chop the carrot and celery as finely as you can so they'll melt into the sauce.

BASIL & THYME ROASTED ONIONS WITH SQUASH, GOAT CHEESE & WALNUTS

This lovely autumnal dish looks beautiful when brought to the table; it's the favorite of this book's designer, Pene. Serve with a green salad and good bread.

Serves: 4
Prep: 10 minutes
Cook: 50 minutes

1⅓ pounds [600g] butternut squash, peeled and cut into ½-inch [1cm] chunks
4 medium yellow onions, halved
1 tablespoon olive oil
1 teaspoon sea salt
Freshly ground black pepper
4 cloves of garlic, unpeeled and halved
8 fresh basil leaves
A handful of fresh thyme sprigs
4½ ounces [125g] soft goat cheese (without rind)
A handful of toasted walnuts, roughly chopped

DRESSING
¾ cup [30g] fresh basil, very finely chopped
3 tablespoons olive oil
1 teaspoon sea salt
½ tablespoon lemon juice

1. Preheat the oven to 425°F [220°C]. Arrange the butternut squash and onions in a single layer in a roasting pan, arranging the onions cut side up. Mix everything well with the olive oil, then sprinkle with the sea salt and black pepper.

2. Top each halved onion with half a clove of garlic, a basil leaf, and a sprig of thyme, and scatter the remaining thyme over the squash. Transfer to the oven and roast for 40–50 minutes, depending on onion size.

3. Remove the dish from the oven and roughly break the goat cheese over the onions and squash in large chunks, making sure each onion gets a piece of cheese over it. Scatter over the walnuts, then return to the oven for an additional 10 minutes, until the onions are soft all the way through when tested with a fork.

4. Meanwhile, for the dressing, mix together the chopped basil, olive oil, sea salt, and lemon juice. When the onions are finished, pour over the dressing and serve hot.

WARMING SWEET POTATO & MUSHROOM POLENTA WITH TOMATOES (V)

I hadn't thought polenta could be baked until I read about it in Alice Hart's *The New Vegetarian*, but now I know it's a wonderful, effort-free way to cook the grain. This recipe is an homage to hers, albeit with garlicky mushrooms and soft, quick-roasted tomatoes as a topping.

Serves: 2
Prep: 10 minutes
Cook: 55 minutes

¾ cup [150g] polenta
1⅔ cups [400ml] vegetable
   stock
3 tablespoons olive oil, divided
⅔ pound [300g] sweet
   potatoes, peeled and cut into
   ¼-inch [5mm] chunks
Freshly ground black pepper
⅔ pound [300g] mini
   portobello or cremini
   mushrooms, sliced
½ pound [200g] cherry
   tomatoes, halved
2 cloves of garlic, crushed
1 teaspoon sea salt

DRESSING
⅓ cup [15g] fresh flat-leaf
   parsley, finely chopped
Juice of 1 lemon
2 tablespoons extra-virgin
   olive oil
½ teaspoon chile flakes

1. Preheat the oven to 400°F [200°C].

2. Line a roasting pan with parchment paper, then add the polenta, vegetable stock, 2 tablespoons of the olive oil, and the sweet potatoes. Stir, season well with black pepper, then transfer to the oven and cook for 40 minutes.

3. Meanwhile, for the dressing, mix together the parsley, lemon juice, extra-virgin olive oil, and chile flakes.

4. In a separate bowl, mix the mushrooms, tomatoes, garlic, sea salt, black pepper, and remaining 1 tablespoon olive oil and set aside.

5. When the polenta has cooked for 40 minutes, take the pan out of the oven and give it a good stir. Top with the mushroom and tomato mixture and return to the oven for an additional 15 minutes, until the mushrooms are softened and the polenta is crisp. Serve with the dressing on the side and a green salad.

3 | SLOW

AN HOUR +
IN THE OVEN

ALL-IN-ONE STICKY RICE WITH BROCCOLI, SQUASH, CHILE & GINGER (V)

BUTTER-ROASTED HARISSA LEEKS & BEETS WITH BULGUR & FETA

GADO GADO: INDONESIAN SALAD WITH WARM POTATOES, GREEN BEANS, BEANSPROUTS & PEANUT-COCONUT DRESSING (V)

ESCALIVADA: SLOW-ROASTED PEPPERS, EGGPLANT & TOMATOES WITH BASIL & ALMOND DRESSING (V)

WHOLE STUFFED MINI PUMPKINS WITH SAGE & GOAT CHEESE

WHOLE ROASTED CAULIFLOWER WITH RAS EL HANOUT, PEARL BARLEY & POMEGRANATE (V)

SWEET POTATO & PARSNIP TAGINE WITH DATES & CILANTRO (V)

HERB-STUFFED ROASTED ONIONS WITH CHERRY TOMATOES & CANNELLINI BEANS

CRUNCHY ROAST POTATO, ARTICHOKE & KALE HASH WITH BAKED EGGS

GROUNDNUT STEW: SWEET POTATOES IN PEANUT & TOMATO SAUCE (V)

3 | SLOW

THREE-BEAN CHILI WITH
AVOCADO SALSA (V)

CAPONATA-STYLE EGGPLANT
WITH OLIVES, CAPERS &
TOMATOES (V)

GENTLY SPICED PEARL BARLEY
WITH TOMATOES, LEEKS, DILL &
PINE NUTS (V)

OVEN-BAKED RATATOUILLE: SLOW-
COOKED ZUCCHINI, EGGPLANT,
PEPPERS & TOMATOES (V)

SWEET POTATOES WITH
TALEGGIO, ONIONS & BASIL

ALL-IN-ONE JEWELED PEARL
BARLEY WITH SQUASH,
POMEGRANATE, WATERCRESS &
FETA

RICH POTATO & MUSHROOM
GRATIN WITH CREAM &
CAMEMBERT

HASSELBACK BUTTERNUT SQUASH
WITH ROASTED ONIONS, LEEKS &
FETA

SIMPLE ALL-IN-ONE DAAL WITH
ROASTED SHALLOTS, CILANTRO,
POMEGRANATE & CASHEWS (V)

ALL-IN-ONE STICKY RICE WITH BROCCOLI, SQUASH, CHILE & GINGER (V)

This sticky coconut rice works perfectly with the sharp cilantro and lime dressing, and the contrasting sweetness of the squash and the crunch from the cashews. It doubles up easily if you're feeding more people.

Serves: 2
Prep: 10 minutes
Cook: 1 hour

$^3/_4$ cup [150g] jasmine rice
One 14.5-ounce [400ml] can coconut milk
1 tablespoon soy sauce
1 inch [2.5cm] ginger, grated
1 clove of garlic
$^2/_3$ pound [300g] squash, peeled and cut into $^1/_2$-inch [1cm] cubes
$^2/_3$ pound [300g] broccoli, cut into florets
3 tablespoons [30g] cashews, to serve

DRESSING
2 tablespoons sesame oil
2 tablespoons lime juice
2 tablespoons soy sauce
1 inch [2.5cm] ginger, grated
1 red chile, finely chopped
$^1/_2$ cup [20g] fresh cilantro, finely chopped

1. Preheat the oven to 400°F [200°C].

2. Mix the rice, coconut milk, soy sauce, ginger, and garlic in a small roasting pan and top with the squash. Cover tightly with foil, then transfer to the oven and cook for 45 minutes.

3. Top the rice and squash with the broccoli, then re-cover and return to the oven for 15 minutes longer. Place the cashew nuts on a small baking sheet and transfer to the oven to toast at the same time.

4. For the dressing, mix together the oil, lime juice, soy sauce, ginger, chile, and cilantro, adjusting the soy and lime juice to taste.

5. Pour the dressing over the hot broccoli, rice, and squash, scatter with the toasted cashews, and serve hot.

Note: Deseed the chile if you prefer a milder dressing.

BUTTER-ROASTED HARISSA LEEKS & BEETS WITH BULGUR & FETA

This tasty all-in-one dish is as good for dinner as it is for lunch the next day. Harissa paste does tend to vary in strength, so try a tiny bit before you start to assess the level of heat, and put a bit more or less in the recipe as you prefer.

Serves: 2 generously
Prep: 10 minutes
Cook: 1 hour

¾ pound [350g] beets, diced into ½-inch [1cm] chunks
2 leeks (about 1 pound [450g]), cut into 1-inch [2.5cm] logs
1–2 tablespoons rose harissa paste
1 tablespoon butter, softened
1 teaspoon sea salt
1¼ cups [200g] bulgur
1⅔ cups [400ml boiling vegetable stock
3½ ounces [100g] feta cheese
A handful of fresh cilantro, roughly chopped
4 tablespoons plain yogurt

1. Preheat the oven to 400°F [200°C].

2. Rub the beets and leeks all over with the harissa paste and butter in a roasting pan. Sprinkle with the sea salt, then transfer to the oven and roast for 45 minutes.

3. Give the vegetables a good stir, then add the bulgur and vegetable stock. Return to the oven for 15 minutes, uncovered.

4. Scatter over the feta cheese and cilantro and serve hot, with the yogurt on the side.

GADO GADO: INDONESIAN SALAD WITH WARM POTATOES, GREEN BEANS, BEAN-SPROUTS & PEANUT-COCONUT DRESSING (V)

This is probably my favorite dish in the book. Roasted potatoes with a spicy peanut dressing and green vegetables—what's not to like? It's been a hit with all my recipe testers, too. It's pretty much a potato salad on acid.

Serves: 2
Prep: 15 minutes
Cook: 1 hour

2¼ pounds [1kg] Yukon gold
    potatoes, halved
2 tablespoons olive oil
1 teaspoon sea salt
½ pound [240g] green beans
⅔ pound [300g] beansprouts
A handful of fresh cilantro,
    to serve

DRESSING
2 tablespoons [50g] crunchy
    peanut butter
⅓ cup [80ml] coconut milk
2 tablespoons lime juice
1½ tablespoons soy sauce
1 fresh red chile, grated
1 inch [2.5cm] ginger, grated

1. Preheat the oven to 400°F [200°C].

2. Mix the potatoes in a roasting pan with the oil and sea salt, then transfer to the oven and cook for 40 minutes.

3. Meanwhile, for the dressing, mix together all the dressing ingredients. Depending on your brand of peanut butter, you may need to add a little more coconut milk so you have a thick, spoonable dressing consistency. Taste and adjust the seasoning as needed.

4. When the potatoes have cooked for 40 minutes, add the green beans and beansprouts. Add a splash more oil if needed, then return to the oven for an additional 20 minutes.

5. Scatter the potatoes and vegetables with the cilantro and serve warm or at room temperature, with the dressing alongside.

    Note: Check the seasoning of the dressing by putting a little bit on a cooked potato and then tasting. Add more soy sauce to the rest of the dressing as needed.

ESCALIVADA: SLOW-ROASTED PEPPERS, EGGPLANT & TOMATOES WITH BASIL & ALMOND DRESSING (V)

This dish reminds me of sitting in an outdoor café in Spain, and it can make even the dullest supermarket produce sing. The quantities given will serve two generously, as that's what fits comfortably into a standard roasting pan, but you can easily double the ingredients and have a veggie feast, maybe even bringing the vegetables to the table whole before "carving" and dressing them.

Serves: 2–3
Prep: 10 minutes
Cook: 1 hour

2 whole eggplants, pricked all
   over with a fork
3 red bell peppers
6 large vine tomatoes
1 red onion, quartered
A handful of fresh thyme sprigs
4 large cloves of garlic,
   unpeeled
1 tablespoon olive oil
2 teaspoons sea salt, divided
$\frac{1}{2}$ cup [50g] whole almonds
1 tablespoon lemon juice
1 tablespoon extra-virgin
   olive oil
$\frac{2}{3}$ cup [25g] fresh basil, roughly
   torn or chopped

TO SERVE
Good crusty bread or pearl
   barley (see page 17)

1. Preheat the oven to 400°F [200°C]. Place the whole eggplants, red bell peppers, vine tomatoes, onion, thyme, garlic, olive oil, and 1 teaspoon of the sea salt into a large roasting pan, then use your hands to coat everything really well in the oil and salt.

2. Transfer to the oven and roast for 1 hour, adding the almonds for the last 10 minutes to toast.

3. Remove the pan from the oven—the vegetables should be charred all over and very soft when poked with a fork. Take out the garlic, and leave the rest of the vegetables to sit while you whisk the lemon juice, extra-virgin olive oil, and remaining 1 teaspoon of sea salt together with the squeezed-out and mashed roasted garlic. Using a knife and fork, remove the inedible tops and stems from the vegetables, then roughly tear apart what remains.

4. Scatter over the basil and the dressing, and mix well. Serve warm, with good crusty bread or pearl barley.

WHOLE STUFFED MINI PUMPKINS
WITH SAGE & GOAT CHEESE

These beautiful little pumpkins are a real showstopper. You can find them in supermarkets around Halloween, or you can use very small squash. They can be very hard to cut, so you will need a sharp, strong knife.

Serves: 4
Prep: 10 minutes
Cook: 1 hour

4 mini pumpkins
Sea salt
16 fresh sage leaves
9 ounces [250g] soft goat cheese
2 teaspoons chile flakes
2$\frac{1}{2}$ tablespoons olive oil, divided
$\frac{1}{2}$ teaspoon chile powder

1. Preheat the oven to 400°F [200°C]. Carefully slice the top off each pumpkin, then, using a small, sharp knife, cut around the cavity containing the seeds. Scoop out the seeds with a spoon and set aside.

2. Season the inside of each cavity with a good pinch of sea salt, then line with two sage leaves. Stuff each with a quarter of the goat cheese, then scatter over the chile flakes before replacing the lid. Rub each pumpkin with $\frac{1}{2}$ tablespoon of the olive oil, scatter with a little more salt, and top each pumpkin with more sage leaves, making sure there's plenty of oil on the leaves too. Transfer to the oven and roast for 1 hour.

3. Rub the pumpkin seeds with a paper towel to get rid of any flesh and then toss with $\frac{1}{2}$ tablespoon of olive oil, the chile powder, and a pinch of sea salt. Ten minutes before the pumpkins are ready, add the seeds to the roasting pan, then return to the oven.

4. Serve the pumpkins whole, with a green salad alongside.

WHOLE ROASTED CAULIFLOWER WITH RAS EL HANOUT, PEARL BARLEY & POMEGRANATE (V)

This is another showstopper of a dish, made with either a whole cauliflower or four little ones. The pearl barley infuses with the spices, creating a harmonious all-in-one dish.

Serves: 4
Prep: 10 minutes
Cook: 1 hour

1½ cups [300g] pearl barley, rinsed
3 cups [700ml] vegetable stock
2 inches [5cm] ginger, grated
1 large cauliflower or 4 mini cauliflowers
2 heaping teaspoons ras el hanout
1 teaspoon sea salt
1 clove of garlic, crushed
2 tablespoons olive oil, divided
¼ pound [100g] spinach, finely chopped
Juice of ½ lemon

TO SERVE
1 pomegranate, seeds only
⅓ cup [40g] toasted almonds
⅔ cup [25g] fresh cilantro, chopped

1. Preheat the oven to 350°F [180°C]. Mix the pearl barley with the vegetable stock and ginger in a deep roasting pan. If using a large cauliflower, remove the leaves, roughly chop them, then stir them in with the pearl barley.

2. Rub the cauliflower all over with the ras el hanout, sea salt, garlic, and 1 tablespoon of the olive oil, then place on top of the pearl barley. Cover the pan tightly with foil, then transfer to the oven to cook for 1 hour.

3. Remove the cauliflower from the pan, then stir in the spinach, lemon juice, and remaining 1 tablespoon olive oil. Season as needed with more salt and lemon juice. Return the cauliflower to the pan, scatter everything with the pomegranate seeds, almonds, and chopped cilantro, and serve hot.

SWEET POTATO & PARSNIP
TAGINE WITH DATES & CILANTRO (V)

Tagines are traditionally "throw-everything-into-the-pot-and-wait" sort of dishes. By all means, use an actual tagine pot if you have one, but a roasting pan covered in foil works just as well. This is sweet and intense—serve with vegan yogurt and flatbreads or couscous.

Serves: 4
Prep: 10 minutes
Cook: 1 hour

1 pound [500g] parsnips, peeled and cut into $\frac{1}{2}$-inch [1cm] slices
1 pound [500g] sweet potatoes, peeled and cut into $\frac{1}{2}$-inch [1cm] half-moons
5 scallions, finely chopped
2 cloves of garlic, crushed
2 inches [5cm] ginger, grated
1 bay leaf
2 heaping teaspoons ras el hanout
1 teaspoon sea salt
10 nice plump dates, halved
One 14.5-ounce [400g] can diced tomatoes
$1\frac{2}{3}$ cups [400ml] vegetable stock
A handful of fresh cilantro, roughly chopped
A handful of toasted almonds

1. Preheat the oven to 400°F [200°C].

2. Add everything except the cilantro and the toasted almonds to a roasting pan, mix well, then cover tightly with foil, transfer to the oven, and roast for 1 hour.

3. Once cooked, give it another stir and taste it for salt, adjusting as needed. Scatter over the cilantro and toasted almonds and serve hot, with couscous or flatbreads.

HERB-STUFFED ROASTED ONIONS WITH CHERRY TOMATOES & CANNELLINI BEANS

In this dish, the onions are stuffed with butter and herbs and roasted whole. They make a lovely simple dinner along with the easy tomato and cannellini bean stew.

Serves: 4
Prep: 10 minutes
Cook: 1 hour

4 red onions
A handful of fresh thyme sprigs
A handful of fresh rosemary
    sprigs
5 tablespoons [75g] butter
One 14.5-ounce [400g] can
    cannellini beans, drained and
    rinsed
$\frac{1}{2}$ pound [200g] cherry
    tomatoes
$\frac{3}{4}$ cup [200ml] vegetable stock
2 bay leaves
Sea salt
Freshly ground black pepper
Juice of $\frac{1}{2}$ lemon
$3\frac{1}{2}$ ounces [100g] feta cheese,
    crumbled
A handful of fresh flat-leaf
    parsley, roughly chopped

1. Preheat the oven to 400°F [200°C]. Cut a tiny section off the end of each onion, so that it sits upright, then cut a deep cross in it, making sure not to cut all the way through. Transfer to a roasting pan, and stuff each one with a few sprigs of thyme and rosemary and a quarter of the butter.

2. Add the cannellini beans, tomatoes, and stock to the pan alongside the onions and add the remaining herbs and the bay leaves. Season the onions and tomatoes well with sea salt and black pepper, then transfer to the oven and roast for 1 hour.

3. Once cooked through, season the cannellini beans with the lemon juice and salt to taste. Scatter over the crumbled feta and parsley and serve hot.

CRUNCHY ROAST POTATO, ARTICHOKE & KALE HASH WITH BAKED EGGS

This is as good for a weekend breakfast as it is for a warming dinner: all your food groups in one gloriously crisp, eggy hash. The chile yogurt brings everything together and you could scatter it with chopped cilantro or any other soft herbs to finish if you wish.

Serves: 4
Prep: 10 minutes
Cook: 1 hour

1¾ pounds [800g] Yukon gold potatoes, peeled and cut into 1-inch [2.5cm] chunks
Two 10-ounce [280g] jars artichokes, drained (reserve the oil)
2 tablespoons oil from the artichokes
2 cloves of garlic, crushed
2 teaspoons sea salt
A good grind of black pepper
½ pound [200g] kale, roughly sliced
4 eggs
½ tablespoon sriracha or your favorite hot chile sauce
3 tablespoons plain yogurt

1. Preheat the oven to 425°F [220°C].

2. Mix the potatoes, artichokes, oil, garlic, sea salt, and black pepper in a roasting pan, then transfer to the oven and roast for 50 minutes.

3. Reduce the heat to 340°F [170°C], and remove the pan from the oven. Stir in the kale, then create four indentations in the vegetables and crack an egg into each one. Season the eggs with a little salt, then return to the oven for an additional 10 minutes, until the whites of the eggs are just set.

4. Meanwhile, mix the chile sauce with the plain yogurt. Serve alongside the eggs and potatoes as soon as they're out of the oven.

GROUNDNUT STEW: SWEET POTATOES IN PEANUT & TOMATO SAUCE (V)

I hadn't had a groundnut stew before trying the one in Ruby Tandoh's *Flavour*, and I found the combination of peanut, tomato, and chile in a sauce addictive—it's my most requested dinner at home. This vegan version, with chunky sweet potatoes and onions, is a good alternative. Serve it with a bowl of freshly cooked white rice.

Serves: 4
Prep: 10 minutes
Cook: 1 hour

2¼ pounds [1kg] sweet potatoes, peeled and cut into ½-inch [1cm] slices
1 yellow onion, roughly sliced
1 inch [2.5cm] ginger, grated
2 cloves of garlic, crushed
1 Scotch bonnet chile, pierced
1 tablespoon olive oil
1 teaspoon sea salt
2 tablespoons [50g] peanut butter
One 14.5-ounce [400g] can diced tomatoes
1⅔ cups [400ml] vegetable stock

TO SERVE
A handful of fresh cilantro, chopped
A handful of salted peanuts, roughly chopped
White rice (see page 17)

1. Preheat the oven to 400°F [200°C].

2. Mix the sweet potatoes, onion, ginger, garlic, and Scotch bonnet with the oil and sea salt in a roasting pan, then transfer to the oven and cook for 45 minutes, until the sweet potatoes are just soft when poked with a fork.

3. Mix together the peanut butter, diced tomatoes, and vegetable stock, and pour over the roasted sweet potatoes. Give everything a good stir, then return to the oven for an additional 15 minutes.

4. Fish out the Scotch bonnet, season the stew to taste with salt, and scatter over the chopped cilantro and peanuts. Serve with hot rice.

THREE-BEAN CHILI
WITH AVOCADO SALSA (V)

This hearty, low-effort chili is perfect by itself or with the chipotle-roasted corn (see page 142).

Serves: 4
Prep: 10 minutes
Cook: 1 hour

½ pound [250g] cremini
   mushrooms, quartered
1 yellow onion, roughly chopped
1 red bell pepper, deseeded and
   roughly chopped
2 teaspoons ground cilantro
2 teaspoons ground cumin
1 teaspoon chipotle chile flakes
1 teaspoon smoked paprika
1 teaspoon sea salt
1 tablespoon olive oil
One 14.5-ounce [400g] can
   cannellini beans
One 14.5-ounce [400g] can
   black beans
One 14.5-ounce [400g] can red
   kidney beans
Two 14.5-ounce [400g] cans
   diced tomatoes
¾ cup [200ml] vegetable stock

SALSA
1 avocado, roughly chopped
Juice of 1 lime
½ red onion, finely chopped
1 teaspoon sea salt

TO SERVE
Cilantro leaves, to garnish
Coconut yogurt
Tortillas or corn chips

1. Preheat the oven to 400°F [200°C].

2. Mix the mushrooms, onion, and red bell pepper with the spices, sea salt, and olive oil in a large, deep roasting pan. Transfer to the oven and roast for 25 minutes.

3. Drain and rinse all the beans and add to the pan with the diced tomatoes and stock. Give everything a good stir, then return to the oven and cook for 35 minutes longer.

4. Just before the chili is ready, for the salad, mix the chopped avocado with the lime juice, red onion, and sea salt to taste. Serve the chili topped with the avocado salsa and cilantro leaves, and with yogurt and tortillas or corn chips alongside.

Note: Stand well away from the oven and watch out for steam when you take the chili out.

CAPONATA-STYLE EGGPLANT WITH OLIVES, CAPERS & TOMATOES (V)

This is the sort of dish you could eat straight from the pan—gloriously tomatoey, and with so much flavor from the capers and olives. Use baby eggplants if you can get them—if not, ordinary eggplant sliced into eighths work well.

Serves: 4
Prep: 10 minutes
Cook: 1 hour

1$\frac{3}{4}$ pounds [800g] baby
   eggplants
1 red onion, cut into eighths
2 tablespoons olive oil
2 teaspoons sea salt
2 cloves of garlic, crushed
3 sprigs of fresh rosemary
3 tablespoons [25g] capers
$\frac{1}{2}$ cup [75g] pitted green olives
One 14.5-ounce [400g] can
   diced tomatoes
2 teaspoons red wine vinegar
$\frac{2}{3}$ cup [25g] fresh basil, torn
$\frac{1}{4}$ cup [30g] toasted almonds

TO SERVE
Bulgur (see page 16) or
   focaccia

1. Preheat the oven to 400°F [200°C].

2. Slice the baby eggplants lengthwise, leaving the stems intact, then transfer to a roasting pan along with the onion. Rub everything well with the olive oil, sea salt, and garlic, and top with the rosemary. Transfer to the oven and roast for 40 minutes.

3. Add the capers, olives, canned tomatoes, and red wine vinegar, stir gently, then return to the oven to cook for an additional 20 minutes, until the sauce has reduced down. Taste and adjust the seasoning as needed. Scatter over the torn basil and almonds and serve with bulgur or focaccia.

GENTLY SPICED PEARL BARLEY
WITH TOMATOES, LEEKS,
DILL & PINE NUTS (V)

This all-in-one pearl barley dish is like a light risotto: warming and full of flavor. It's impressive enough to serve at a potluck for friends, and comforting enough for a TV dinner with a glass of (red) wine and an episode of *Scandal*.

Serves: 4
Prep: 10 minutes
Cook: 1 hour

1 pound [450g] vine tomatoes, chopped
2 leeks, thinly sliced
2 cloves of garlic, grated
1 teaspoon chile flakes
1 teaspoon sea salt
2 bay leaves
1½ cups [300g] pearl barley
3 cups [700ml] vegetable stock
1 tablespoon olive oil

DRESSING
1 tablespoon lemon juice
2 tablespoons extra-virgin olive oil
1 teaspoon sea salt
Freshly ground black pepper
3½ tablespoons [25g] fresh dill, roughly chopped

TO SERVE
⅓ cup [40g] toasted pine nuts

1. Preheat the oven to 425°F [220°C].

2. Mix the tomatoes, leeks, garlic, chile flakes, salt, bay leaves, pearl barley, stock, and olive oil in a deep roasting pan or casserole dish and cover tightly with foil or a lid. Transfer to the oven and cook for 1 hour.

3. Meanwhile, for the dressing, whisk together the lemon juice, extra-virgin olive oil, sea salt, black pepper, and dill in a small bowl and set aside.

4. Once the pearl barley is cooked, stir in the dill dressing and season to taste with additional salt, pepper, and lemon juice. Serve scattered with the pine nuts.

OVEN-BAKED RATATOUILLE: SLOW-COOKED ZUCCHINI, EGGPLANT, PEPPERS & TOMATOES (V)

The trick with this ratatouille is to cut the zucchini really thinly, so it absorbs all the flavors from the sauce. This is lovely on the day it is made, but even better the next day, warmed in the oven, so if you're in the mood for a bit of batch cooking for the week ahead, this is your dish.

Serves: 4
Prep: 10 minutes
Cook: 1 hour

2 large zucchini, very thinly sliced
I large eggplant, sliced into $\frac{1}{4}$-inch [5mm] half-moons
2 red bell peppers, deseeded and roughly chopped
1 red onion, roughly chopped
2 cloves of garlic, crushed
2 tablespoons olive oil
2 heaping teaspoons sea salt
Freshly ground black pepper
$\frac{2}{3}$ cup [25g] fresh basil, roughly chopped
Two 14.5-ounce [400g] cans diced tomatoes
$1\frac{1}{4}$ cups [75g] fresh white breadcrumbs
1 ounce [30g] vegan Parmesan, grated

TO SERVE
Crusty bread

1. Preheat the oven to 400°F [200°C].

2. Mix the vegetables, garlic, oil, sea salt, black pepper, and basil in a medium-size roasting pan or lasagna dish, then top with the canned tomatoes. Smooth the tomatoes over the vegetables, then transfer to the oven and roast for 30 minutes.

3. Remove the pan from the oven and increase the heat to 425°F [220°C]. Give the vegetables a stir, then top with the breadcrumbs and Parmesan and return to the oven for an additional 30 minutes.

4. Leave the ratatouille to cool down for 10–15 minutes, then serve with plenty of crusty bread.

Note: Don't panic if it looks like there's too much liquid in the pan after the first 30 minutes; it will absorb perfectly by the end.

SWEET POTATOES WITH TALEGGIO, ONIONS & BASIL

My friend Laura reinvented sweet potatoes when we were roommates. She perfected softening a combination of finely chopped red onions and garlic that we then piled into the hot potatoes, along with a good dollop of Greek yogurt. This version, with rich Taleggio and a basil dressing, is perfect comfort food.

Serves: 4
Prep: 15 minutes
Cook: 1 hour

4 sweet potatoes (about
    2¼ pounds [1kg])
2 red onions, quartered
1 tablespoon olive oil
1 teaspoon sea salt
A handful of lemon thyme
    sprigs
7 ounces [200g] Taleggio,
    thickly sliced

DRESSING
¾ cup [30g] fresh basil, very
    finely chopped
3 tablespoons olive oil
1 clove of garlic, finely grated
1 teaspoon sea salt
½ tablespoon lemon juice

1. Preheat the oven to 400°F [200°C].

2. Prick the sweet potatoes all over with a fork, then add them to a roasting pan with the quartered onions. Rub the potatoes and onions with the oil and sea salt, then scatter over the lemon thyme. Transfer to the oven and roast for 55 minutes.

3. For the dressing, mix the chopped basil with the olive oil, garlic, sea salt, and lemon juice and set aside.

4. When the sweet potatoes have cooked for 55 minutes, take the pan out of the oven and cut a cross into each potato—they should be wonderfully soft inside. Lay the slices of Taleggio inside the potatoes, then return to the oven for an additional 5 minutes for the cheese to melt. Serve hot, with the onions and dressing alongside.

ALL-IN-ONE JEWELED PEARL BARLEY WITH SQUASH, POMEGRANATE, WATERCRESS & FETA

This is a vibrant, elegant dinner: the pearl barley cooks beautifully in the oven alongside the squash, with the fresh elements added just at the end. It's excellent for lunch the next day, too.

Serves: 4
Prep: 15 minutes
Cook: 1 hour

1$\frac{2}{3}$-pounds [750g] butternut squash, peeled and cut into $\frac{1}{2}$-inch [1cm] chunks
All the seeds from the squash (or a handful of pumpkin seeds, if that's easier)
Sea salt
1 teaspoon olive oil
1$\frac{1}{2}$ cups [300g] pearl barley, rinsed
3 cups [700ml] boiling vegetable stock
2 cloves of garlic, crushed
1 4-ounce [100g] bag of watercress, roughly chopped
1 tablespoon lime juice
1 tablespoon extra-virgin olive oil
3$\frac{1}{2}$ ounces [100g] feta cheese, crumbled
1 pomegranate, seeds only
Freshly ground black pepper

1. Preheat the oven to 425°F [220°C]. Place the butternut squash chunks into the roasting pan, then spread the seeds you've saved from the squash on another baking sheet and rub with a pinch of sea salt and the olive oil.

2. Mix the pearl barley, vegetable stock, and crushed garlic with the squash chunks, then cover tightly with foil and transfer to the oven to cook for 1 hour. Add the baking sheet with the seeds to the oven after 50 minutes.

3. When the squash and pearl barley have cooked for an hour, remove both trays from the oven and stir in the watercress, lime juice, and extra-virgin olive oil.

4. Top with the feta, pomegranate seeds, and toasted squash seeds. Season with sea salt and black pepper to taste and serve hot.

RICH POTATO & MUSHROOM GRATIN WITH CREAM & CAMEMBERT

Somewhere between a tartiflette and a dauphinoise, this rich gratin takes elements from both and combines them for a very satisfying, if heavy, winter dish (I have been known to have leftovers for breakfast). Serve with a green salad.

Serves: 6
Prep: 15 minutes
Cook: 1 hour

2$\frac{1}{4}$ pounds [1kg] Yukon gold potatoes, sliced paper thin
1 onion, finely sliced
$\frac{2}{3}$ pound [300g] cremini mushrooms, thinly sliced
Sea salt
Freshly ground black pepper
Freshly ground nutmeg
2 cloves of garlic, grated
3$\frac{1}{3}$ cups [800ml] heavy cream
8$\frac{1}{4}$ ounces [240g] Camembert
10–12 fresh sage leaves

TO SERVE
Green salad

1. Preheat the oven to 400°F [200°C]. Butter a medium-size roasting pan or lasagna dish, then add a layer of potatoes, followed by onions and mushrooms. Season with a generous pinch of sea salt, black pepper, and a grating of nutmeg, then repeat the layers, seasoning between each, and finishing with a layer of potatoes.

2. Mix the garlic with the heavy cream, add another good pinch each of salt, pepper, and grated nutmeg, and then pour it all over the potatoes. Top with the Camembert and sage leaves, then transfer to the oven and cook for 1 hour.

3. Let the gratin sit for 10 minutes, then serve with a crisp green salad alongside.

   Note: It might seem like you're adding a lot of salt, but the potatoes absolutely drink it in; you may even need to serve salt on the table so people can season to taste.

HASSELBACK BUTTERNUT SQUASH WITH ROASTED ONIONS, LEEKS & FETA

Hasselback butternut squash is having its moment in the sun. Its beautiful color makes for a good-looking centerpiece. This dish incorporates leeks, which soften down into a lovely, rich gravy.

Serves: 4
Prep: 15 minutes
Cook: 1 hour 10 minutes

1 medium butternut squash
A handful of fresh rosemary
A handful of fresh thyme sprigs
6 bay leaves
2 red onions, halved crosswise
2 leeks, cut into 1-inch [2.5cm] logs
3½ tablespoons [50g] butter, thinly sliced
1 teaspoon sea salt
1¼ cups [300ml] vegetable stock
4 tablespoons crème fraîche
3½ ounces [100g] feta cheese, crumbled

1. Preheat the oven to 400°F [200°C]. Carefully halve the squash, remove the seeds, then place cut side down on a cutting board. Cut *almost* all the way through the squash, but not quite—you want a series of parallel cuts.

2. Stuff each cut alternately with rosemary, thyme, and bay leaves, then transfer to a roasting pan along with the onions and leeks. Lay the sliced butter over the squash and onions, and season with the sea salt. Pour the stock into the pan, then transfer to the oven and roast for 1 hour 10 minutes.

3. Mash down the softened leeks with a wooden spoon and stir in the crème fraîche. Scatter the crumbled feta over the squash and serve with the onion and leek gravy.

SIMPLE ALL-IN-ONE DAAL
WITH ROASTED SHALLOTS, CILANTRO,
POMEGRANATE & CASHEWS (V)

This easy, flavorful daal will look after itself in the oven for an hour, so you won't need to worry about it running dry. With a little coconut milk or light cream stirred in at the end, it's rich and comforting, and perfect served with rice or naan.

Serves: 4
Prep: 10 minutes
Cook: 1 hour 25 minutes

½ pound [200g] shallots, peeled and halved
1 tablespoon vegetable oil
1 bay leaf
1 teaspoon ground cumin
1 teaspoon ground cilantro
½ teaspoon ground turmeric
1 teaspoon freshly ground black pepper
1 cup [225g] brown lentils, rinsed well
3 cups [700ml] boiling water
2 inches [5cm] ginger, grated
2 cloves of garlic, crushed
2 teaspoons sea salt
⅔ cup [150ml] coconut milk or light cream
Juice of 1 lime

TO SERVE
1 pomegranate, seeds only
A handful of fresh cilantro, roughly chopped
A handful of toasted cashews

1. Preheat the oven to 400°F [200°C].

2. Place the shallots into a small, deep roasting pan and mix well with the vegetable oil, bay leaf, and spices. Transfer to the oven and roast for 25 minutes.

3. After 25 minutes, add the rinsed lentils, boiling water, ginger, and garlic to the pan. Give everything a good stir, then cover tightly with foil and return to the oven for 1 hour.

4. When the lentils have cooked for an hour, season generously with the salt and stir in the coconut milk or light cream. Taste and add lime juice and more salt as needed. Scatter over the pomegranate seeds, cilantro, and cashews, and serve with rice or naan.

DIY
INFOGRAPHICS

DRESS

OLIVE OIL

BLACK PEPPER

SEA SALT

ACIDITY

LEMON

POMEGRANATE MOLASSES

LIME

VINEGAR

ADD

FRESH

ORANGE

AVOCADO

GRAPEFRUIT

POMEGRANATE SEEDS

TOMATO

APPLE

PROTEIN

GOAT CHEESE

ALMONDS

GORGONZOLA PICCANTE

CASHEWS

FETA

ROAST

OLIVE OIL

SEA SALT

VEGETABLES

CELERY ROOT

BEET

BUTTERNUT SQUASH

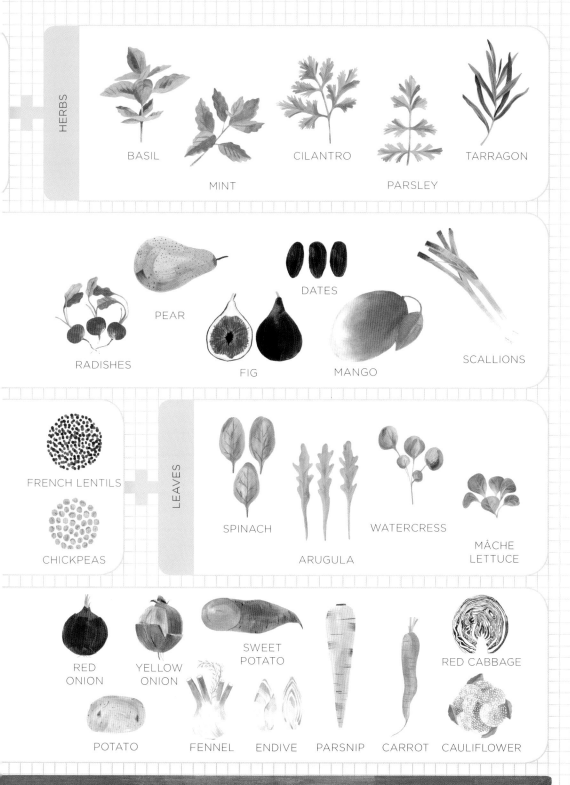

HERBS

BASIL

MINT

CILANTRO

PARSLEY

TARRAGON

RADISHES

PEAR

DATES

FIG

MANGO

SCALLIONS

FRENCH LENTILS

CHICKPEAS

LEAVES

SPINACH

ARUGULA

WATERCRESS

MÂCHE
LETTUCE

RED
ONION

YELLOW
ONION

SWEET
POTATO

RED CABBAGE

POTATO

FENNEL

ENDIVE

PARSNIP

CARROT

CAULIFLOWER

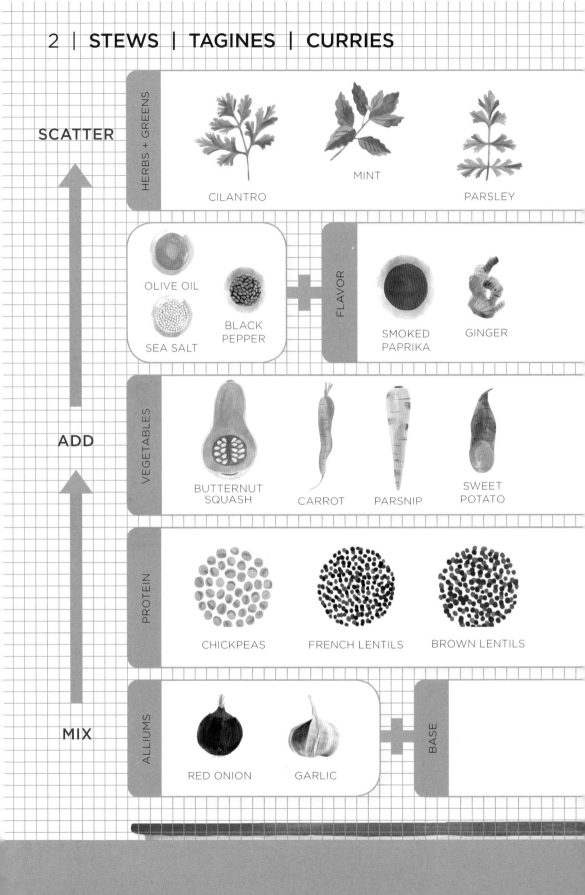

SCATTER

ADD

MIX

HERBS + GREENS

CILANTRO

MINT

PARSLEY

OLIVE OIL

SEA SALT

BLACK PEPPER

FLAVOR

SMOKED PAPRIKA

GINGER

VEGETABLES

BUTTERNUT SQUASH

CARROT

PARSNIP

SWEET POTATO

PROTEIN

CHICKPEAS

FRENCH LENTILS

BROWN LENTILS

ALLIUMS

RED ONION

GARLIC

BASE

WATERCRESS

SCALLIONS

SPINACH

ARUGULA

CHILE

CILANTRO
SEEDS

RAS EL HANOUT

CUMIN
SEEDS

MAKRUT
LIME

LEMONGRASS

CELERY
ROOT

OKRA

FENNEL

BEET

LEEK

CANNELLINI BEANS

KIDNEY BEANS

BLACK BEANS

CRANBERRY BEANS

COCONUT MILK

CANNED TOMATOES

VEGETABLE STOCK

DRESS

HERBS

BASIL

DILL

THYME

CHEESE

GOAT CHEESE

FETA

MOZZARELLA

OVEN

VEGETABLES—SLICED OR CUBED

BROCCOLI

CAULIFLOWER

BRUSSELS SPROUTS

CELERY
ROOT

BUTTERNUT
SQUASH

EGGPLANT

BEET

LAYER

BASE

SEA SALT

BLACK
PEPPER

+

PASTRY DOUGH

ROSEMARY

OREGANO

PARSLEY

PARMESAN

GORGONZOLA
PICCANTE

CHEDDAR

FENNEL

MUSHROOM

POTATO

RED BELL
PEPPER

ZUCCHINI

ALLIUMS

RED ONION

YELLOW
ONION

LEEK

GARLIC

SCALLIONS

CRÈME
FRAÎCHE

YOGURT

HEAVY CREAM

VEGETABLE STOCK

4 | SUPERGRAIN TRAY

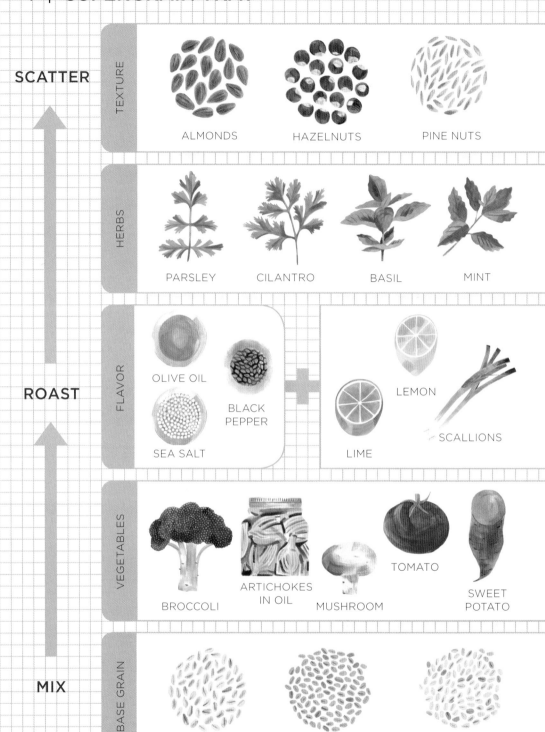

SCATTER

ROAST

MIX

TEXTURE

ALMONDS HAZELNUTS PINE NUTS

HERBS

PARSLEY CILANTRO BASIL MINT

FLAVOR

OLIVE OIL

BLACK PEPPER

SEA SALT

LEMON

LIME

SCALLIONS

VEGETABLES

BROCCOLI

ARTICHOKES IN OIL

MUSHROOM

TOMATO

SWEET POTATO

BASE GRAIN

PEARL BARLEY SPELT BULGUR

PISTACHIOS

PEANUTS

WALNUTS

CASHEWS

THYME

ROSEMARY

SPINACH

WATERCRESS

ARUGULA

CHILE

GARLIC

HARISSA PASTE

GINGER

RAS EL HANOUT

CILANTRO SEEDS

CUMIN SEEDS

SUMAC

BUTTERNUT SQUASH

KALE

ASPARAGUS

BEET

FENNEL

FARRO

BUCKWHEAT

BROWN RICE

ORZO

RECIPE
PAIRINGS

RECIPE
PAIRINGS

INDIAN FEASTS

SPICED ROASTED CARROT & BEAN CURRY (V)	76
BEET, CHICKPEA & COCONUT CURRY (V)	146
CRISPY TAMARIND SPROUTS WITH PEANUTS & SHALLOTS (V)	62
OKRA & CHICKPEA CURRY WITH ALMONDS (V)	130
SIMPLE ALL-IN-ONE DAAL WITH ROASTED SHALLOTS, CILANTRO, POMEGRANATE & CASHEWS (V)	195
SQUASH & SPINACH CURRY (V)	131

SOUTHEAST ASIAN DINNER

ROASTED CABBAGE QUARTERS WITH SICHUAN PEPPER, SESAME & MUSHROOMS (V)	56
SMOKED TOFU WITH FENNEL, BOK CHOY & PEANUT SATAY DRESSING (V)	24
MISO EGGPLANT WITH TOFU, SESAME & CHILE (V)	140
LIME & CILANTRO MUSHROOMS WITH BOK CHOY & ASPARAGUS (V)	30
GADO GADO: INDONESIAN SALAD WITH WARM POTATOES, GREEN BEANS, BEANSPROUTS & PEANUT-COCONUT DRESSING (V)	162
ALL-IN-ONE STICKY RICE WITH BROCCOLI, SQUASH, CHILE & GINGER (V)	158

LIGHT LUNCHES

LUNCHBOX PASTA SALAD: QUICK-ROAST BROCCOLI
WITH OLIVES, SUN-DRIED TOMATOES, BASIL & PINE NUTS (V)   60

ROASTED RED CABBAGE WITH CRISP GARLIC CROUTONS,
APPLES, RAISINS & MÂCHE LETTUCE (V)   50

CARROT & TALEGGIO TARTE TATIN   96

ROSEMARY ROASTED ENDIVE & RADISH SALAD
WITH ASPARAGUS & ORANGE (V)   72

MIDDLE EASTERN TABLE

ROASTED CAULIFLOWER WITH CHICKPEAS, KALE,
LEMON & TAHINI (V)   90

PERSIAN MUSHROOMS WITH POMEGRANATE & WALNUTS (V)   139

WHOLE ROASTED CAULIFLOWER WITH RAS EL HANOUT,
PEARL BARLEY & POMEGRANATE (V)   170

EGGPLANT WITH TOMATOES, HARISSA & ALMONDS (V)   132

ALL-IN-ONE JEWELED PEARL BARLEY WITH SQUASH,
POMEGRANATE, WATERCRESS & FETA   190

CRISP CAULIFLOWER STEAKS WITH HARISSA & GOAT CHEESE   68

SOUTH AMERICAN POTLUCK

FAJITA-SPICED MUSHROOMS & PEPPERS WITH STILTON & SOUR CREAM	26
THREE-BEAN CHILI WITH AVOCADO SALSA (V)	178
CHIPOTLE ROASTED CORN WITH SQUASH, BLACK BEANS, FETA & LIME	142

Note: Make the chili ahead because the oven will get too steamy for the corn to roast if you try to cook both dishes at the same time.

AUTUMNAL DINNERS

GENTLY SPICED PEARL BARLEY WITH TOMATOES, LEEKS, DILL & PINE NUTS (V)	184
SWEET DREAMS ARE MADE OF GREENS (V) *(omit the quinoa)*	32
CREOLE-SPICED LEEK & MUSHROOM TART	98
BASIL & THYME ROASTED ONIONS WITH SQUASH, GOAT CHEESE & WALNUTS	150
WHOLE STUFFED MINI PUMPKINS WITH SAGE & GOAT CHEESE	168
QUICK-ROASTED FENNEL & BULGUR WITH MOZZARELLA, FIGS, POMEGRANATE & DILL	46

WEEKEND LUNCHES

LEEK & FRENCH LENTIL GRATIN
WITH CRUNCHY FETA TOPPING   124

WATERCRESS & PARSNIP PANZANELLA
WITH GORGONZOLA, HONEY & RADISHES   74

RED WINE MUSHROOM CASSEROLE
WITH CHEESE COBBLER TOPPING   118

HONEY-ROASTED ROOT VEGETABLE SALAD
WITH BLUE CHEESE & SPINACH   134

SQUASH & GORGONZOLA TART WITH FIGS & PECANS   102

LUXE WARM WINTER SALAD: ROASTED POTATOES & CELERY ROOT
WITH TRUFFLE, PARMESAN & SOFT-BOILED EGGS   136

PICNIC TABLE

THE MOST INDULGENT QUICK-COOK QUICHE;
BROCCOLI, GORGONZOLA, CHILE & WALNUT   92

ROASTED TOMATO, RED BELL PEPPER & ARTICHOKE PANZANELLA
WITH TARRAGON & LEMON (V)   116

HERBY ROASTED PEPPERS STUFFED
WITH ARTICHOKES, OLIVES & FETA   112

RAINBOW TABBOULEH WITH AVOCADO,
RADISHES & POMEGRANATE (V)   42

INDEX

ACKNOWLEDGMENTS

Cookbooks are always a collaborative process, and I was delighted to have the same team on this book as for the last. Thanks are owed to Rowan Yapp, Harriet Dobson and the team at Square Peg for taking on another book and for their patience and support throughout the writing and testing, and to Pene Parker for the beautiful design, art direction, and help on the shoot. I was incredibly lucky to work with the brilliant David Loftus again on the photographs for the book; thank you so much for making it look wonderful, and for your and Ange's amazing support. Grace Helmer—the illustrations are stunning, thank you so much.

Team Glengyle—what would I do without you? Danielle Adams Norenberg, Christine Beck, Emma Drage, and Laura Hutchinson, thank you so much for the thorough recipe testing, advice, and general brilliance. I've learned so much from all of you, both in and out of the kitchen.

This sort of cookbook isn't a literary masterpiece (though Alice would approve on account of the many pictures and few words), but I'd like to thank Megan Smedley and Vic Northwood for their early encouragement at a time when it was much needed. It was a privilege to be in your classes, and I was extremely lucky to have you both as teachers.

My family—Parvati, Vijay, and Padmini Iyer—are absolutely the best cheerleaders. Ma, thank you so much for your thorough and enthusiastic help recipe testing again; Dad, thank you for your unwavering belief in my abilities; Padz, as tempting as it is to write "Not you!," Boosh style, you are the best. Please can I move into your retirement community? I will do the cooking as long as I don't have to play Gloomhaven.

Ross, the man in my pics: your feedback on every dish in this book was invaluable, from the occasional, slightly pained "This needs work," through to enthusiastic assent and polished-off plates. Thank you for not minding my kitchen takeover; I know you can't wait to go back to using three saucepans, five steamers, one wok, and twelve garlic crushers for every weeknight dinner now that this book is finished. This book is for you.

ABOUT THE AUTHOR

RUKMINI IYER is a food stylist and author of the best-selling cookbook *Dinner's in the Oven: Simple One-Pan Meals*. She loves creating new recipes and working on food photo shoots. When she's not styling, cooking, or entertaining, she can usually be found reading by the riverside, filling her balcony and flat with more plants than they can hold, and planning her dream kitchen garden, complete with pet chickens.

First published in the United States of America in 2019 by
Chronicle Books LLC.
First published in the United Kingdom in 2017 by Square Peg,
an imprint of Random House UK.

Library of Congress Cataloging-in-Publication Data:

Names: Iyer, Rukmini, author. | Loftus, David, photographer.
Title: Vegetarian Dinner's in the Oven : one-pan vegetarian and
   vegan recipes / by Rukmini Iyer ; photographs by David Loftus.
Other titles: Dinner's in the oven. Vegetarian
Description: San Francisco : Chronicle Books, 2019. | "First published
   in the United Kingdom in 2017 by Square Peg." | Includes index.
Identifiers: LCCN 2018021681 | ISBN 9781452176987 (hardcover :
   alk. paper)
Subjects: LCSH: Vegetarian cooking. | Vegan cooking. | Roasting
   (Cooking) | One-dish meals. | LCGFT: Cookbooks.
Classification: LCC TX837.I94 2019 | DDC 641.5/636—dc23
   LC record available at https://lccn.loc.gov/2018021681

Manufactured in China

Design by Pene Parker
Prop Styling by Pene Parker
Food Styling by Rukmini Iyer
Illustrations by Grace Helmer

10 9 8 7 6 5 4 3 2 1

Chronicle books and gifts are available at special quantity discounts
to corporations, professional associations, literacy programs, and
other organizations. For details and discount information, please
contact our corporate/premiums department at corporatesales@
chroniclebooks.com or at 1-800-759-0190.

Chronicle Books LLC
680 Second Street
San Francisco, California 94107
www.chroniclebooks.com